Gulliver's
Travels

AN ADAPTED CLASSIC

Gulliver's Travels

Jonathan Swift

GLOBE FEARON

Pearson Learning Group

Executive Editor: Barbara Levadi
Adapter: T. Ernesto Bethancourt
Senior Editor: Bernice Golden
Assistant Editor: Roger Weisman
Art Director: Nancy Sharkey
Cover Illustration and Interior Illustrations: Steve Moore
Production Editor: Linda Greenberg
Electronic Systems Specialist: José López
Marketing Manager: Sandra Hutchison

ISBN 0-8359-0853-4
Printed in the United States of America

11 12 13   06 07 08 09

1-800-321-3106
www.pearsonlearning.com

CONTENTS

ABOUT THE AUTHOR

Jonathan Swift was born to English parents in Dublin, Ireland, on November 30, 1667. His father, a lawyer, died before young Jonathan was born. His mother returned to England while he was a child. She left young Swift in the care of his uncle, Godwin, who provided Jonathan with a good education. He went to Kilkenny School and Trinity College in Ireland. He earned a master's degree at age 21.

During that year, 1688, there was an uprising in Scotland, backed by the French king. England had been officially Protestant since the time of Henry VIII. This rebellion attempted to make England a Roman Catholic country again. In addition, political parties were each trying to gain control of the government.

Young Jonathan wanted to be where the action was. Through some family connections, he became secretary to Sir William Temple, who was one of the leading Whig politicians. Temple also had a great private library. In the England of the 1600s, there were no public libraries. Only the rich had libraries, and most people couldn't read or write.

Swift studied and wrote about the great works of literature. Because he was a politician's secretary, he also was able to view close up how politics worked. His experiences gave Swift the background for his political satires.

In a pamphlet entitled *A Modest Proposal*, written in 1729, Swift attacked England's hypocrisy and the oppression of the Irish people. In *Gulliver's Travels*, Swift pokes fun at English life. What makes this novel so effective is its humor and bitter sarcasm. Politicians and the nobility usually expect to be insulted. It comes with the job. What they cannot tolerate is to be laughed at. In *Gulliver*, Swift stepped on some very powerful toes.

Because of this, Swift didn't dare publish *Gulliver* under his own name. It could have been argued that parts of this book were treason, and treason was punishable by death.

The book caused a great stir in both England and Ireland. It was also a tremendous success. Like it or hate it, every politician and noble read it. In many places, they recognized themselves in disguise. It was Swift's good luck that the causes he argued for were the right ones.

When William and Mary sat on the throne of England, the government settled down. Swift stayed in Ireland for the rest of his life. He visited England only twice. He was greatly respected, though he still had many political enemies. He never married.

On his tomb, in Ireland, he wrote his own epitaph, as Shakespeare had done years before him. It says simply that he had fought for liberty for all men. No one can deny that his efforts changed English and Irish history. In a sense, *Gulliver's Travels* shows how he fought. He used the most powerful of all weapons: his pen and his wit.

PREFACE

The early 1700s was a time when there was a demand for great social, political, and economic changes in England and Ireland. One must remember that the American Revolution and the Bill of Rights, guaranteeing freedom of the press, were still 50 years away. If an author or reformer was not careful, he could have his work suppressed or even be jailed.

The fictional lands that Gulliver visited really represent England. The outrageous characters and bizarre situations that Swift invented are really barbs directed at familiar figures in the English government and society at that time. Above all, he made fun of these figures. Laughter and ridicule are two of the most powerful tools for social reform. This way of exposing and criticizing wrongdoings, abuses, and stupidities is called *satire*. Satire can take the form of stories, poems, or plays. Satire's purpose is to make people stop and think about foolishness and injustices—with the hope that people will demand social change.

If anyone in power came down on Swift, he could say that he was writing about imaginary countries and people of his own invention. Swift's outrageous inventions included the tiny people of Lilliput, the giants of Brobdingnag, and the horse people of the land of Houyhnmn.

Swift's observations about the hearts and ways of people remain as true today. Greed, pride, poverty, poor government, and social injustice are still with us more than 200 years later. One may read *Gulliver's Travels* as history, social satire, or the great tale of adventure that it still is. It is, by turns, exciting, sad, biting, and above all, funny.

ADAPTER'S NOTE

In preparing this edition of *Gulliver's Travels,* we have kept the author's main purpose in mind. However, language has changed since the book was originally published. We have changed some of Swift's vocabulary and shortened and simplified many of his sentences and paragraphs. We have, however, kept as much of Swift's original style as possible.

PEOPLE AND PLACES IN
GULLIVER'S TRAVELS

PART ONE: A VOYAGE TO LILLIPUT

LEMUEL GULLIVER

Tells the story of Gulliver's Travels; *an Englishman and a doctor*

GOLBASTO MOMAREN EVLAME GURDILO SHEFIN
MULLY ULLY GUE

The emperor of Lilliput

FLIMNAP

The treasurer of Lilliput

RELDRESAL

A nobleman of Lilliput and friend to Gulliver

SKYRESH BOLGOLAM

Lilliputian Secretary of the Navy

SLAMECKSAN

The "low heels" Lilliputian political party

TRAMECKSAN

The "high heels" Lilliputian political party

NARDAC

A Lilliputian person of nobility; Gulliver becomes a Nardac for capturing the Blefuscudian navy.

LILLIPUT

A Pacific Ocean island near Tasmania

BLEFUSCU

An island of little people located across a strait from Lilliput

PART TWO: A VOYAGE TO BROBDINGNAG

JOHN NICHOLAS

The captain of the Adventure, *the ship that brought Gulliver to Brobdingnag*

BROBDINGNAG

A land on an Asian peninsula, inhabited by a race of giants

GLUMDALCLITCH

A giant farmer's daughter, who becomes Gulliver's nurse and protector

SPLACKNUCK

A man-like creature, native to Brobdingnag; Gulliver is mistaken for one of these animals.

THOMAS WILCOCKS

The captain of the ship that rescues Gulliver after he is dropped in the sea by a giant eagle

PART THREE: A VOYAGE TO LAPUTA

LAPUTA

A flying island, populated by a race of super geniuses

FLAPPERS

Servants of the Laputan, who get their masters' attention by hitting them with inflated bladders

BALNIBARBI

A slave state of Laputa, whose people must do the bidding of Laputa or be bombed

GLUBBDUBDRIB

An island of wizards, part of the kingdom of Luggnagg

LUGGNAGG

An island kingdom, where some people are immortal

STRULDBRUGGS

A race of people of Luggnagg, who live forever

PART FOUR: A VOYAGE TO HOUYHNHNM LAND

HOUYHNHNMS

A race of horse people, far advanced socially and politically

YAHOOS

A race of man-like creatures, who are naked, filthy, and repulsive

THE HOUYHNHNM MASTER

The horse person who finds Gulliver and keeps him as a pet

THE SORREL NAG

A servant of the Houyhnhnm Master and Gulliver's guardian

THE VERY IMPORTANT HOUYHNHNM

One of the horse people placed high in their government; he passes judgment on Gulliver.

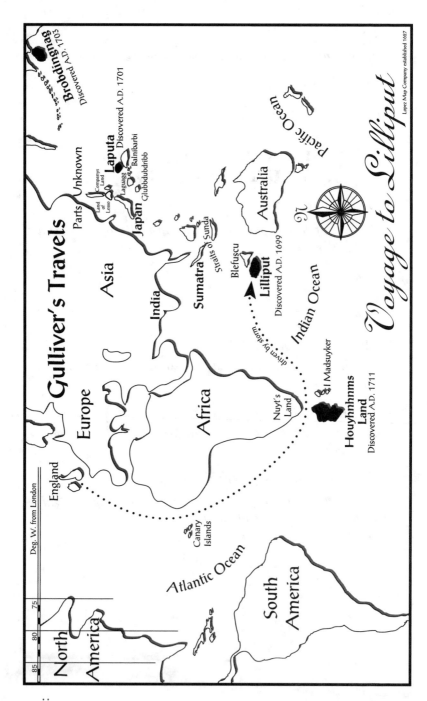

Gulliver's Travels

Voyage to Lilliput

Deg. W. from London

85   80   75

North America

England

Europe

Asia

Parts Unknown

Brobdingnag Discovered A.D. 1703

Laputa Discovered A.D. 1701
Balnibarbi
Laguag
Land of Lesso
Company's Land
Glubbdubdribb

Japan

India

Sumatra

Straits of Sunda

Blefuscu

Lilliput Discovered A.D. 1699

Australia

Pacific Ocean

Indian Ocean

driven by storm

I Madsuyker

Houyhnhnms Land Discovered A.D. 1711

Nuyt's Land

Africa

Canary Islands

Atlantic Ocean

South America

North America

Lopez Map Company established 1697

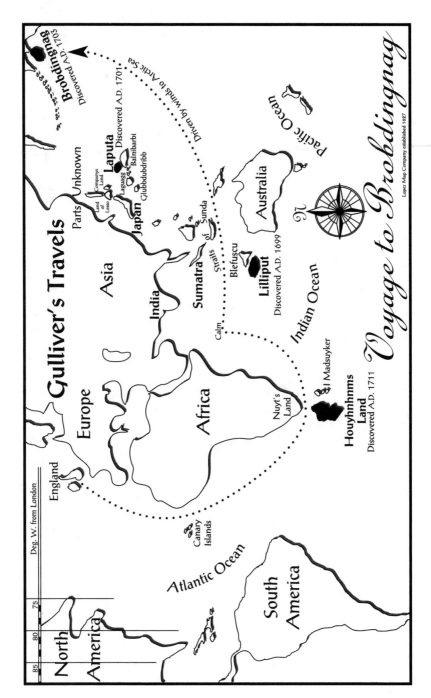

Gulliver's Travels

Voyage to Brobdingnag

Lopez Map Company established 1927

Deg. W. from London

England

Europe

North America

Atlantic Ocean

South America

Canary Islands

Africa

Nuyt's Land

Asia

India

Parts Unknown

Land of Lesse

Company's Land

Laputa
Discovered A.D. 1701

Balnibarbi

Laguagg

Glubbdubdribb

Japan

Sumatra

Straits of Sunda

Blefuscu

Lilliput
Discovered A.D. 1699

Houyhnhnms Land
Discovered A.D. 1711

I Madsuyker

Calm

Indian Ocean

Australia
Discovered A.D. 1699

Pacific Ocean

Driven by winds to Arctic Sea

Brobdingnag
Discovered A.D. 1703

75

80

85

PART ONE:

A VOYAGE TO LILLIPUT

1 Meeting the Tiny Folk

My name is Lemuel Gulliver. I was born in Nottinghamshire, England, the third of five sons. Through good fortune, I was able to complete an education in medicine. I soon discovered that setting up a practice wasn't easy. But I found that merchant ships are always in need of doctors. I shipped out on a craft called the *Swallow*.

I returned with enough money to set up a medical practice. It was then I married Mary Burton. But my medical practice was not doing very well. Once again, I went to sea, this time aboard a ship called the *Antelope*. On May 4, 1699, we set sail from Bristol, bound for the East Indies.

We sailed with good weather down the coast of Africa and around the Cape of Good Hope.[1] But not far from Australia, a terrible storm came up. The *Antelope* was driven onto a reef and began to break up on the rocks. I was trying desperately to launch a small boat when I was washed overboard. I cannot say how long I was in the cold, dark waters. After a time, I began to pass out.

I awoke on dry land, with the sun shining on my face. I do not know how I had made it there safely. In fact, I had no idea where I was. I tried to sit up but found that I could not move. My mind raced through my medical training. Was my back broken? Was I

---

1. Cape of Good Hope the southernmost tip of Africa

paralyzed? It didn't seem likely. I could feel my legs, feet, and hands. Yet, I could not move.

It was then that I realized there were some sort of ties—like strong lengths of string—binding my limbs. The sun was in my eyes, and I tried to move my head. I discovered that my hair, which I wear long, was somehow fastened to the ground. I could hear some small, strange noises around me. I was unable to see what was causing them.

Then I felt something, perhaps a small animal, crawling on my leg. It moved across my chest and almost to my chin. Looking downward, I was amazed at what I saw! It was a tiny man, no taller than six inches. I could have laughed, but he had a tiny bow and arrow in his hands. He also looked ready to use it! In the meantime, I felt what I guessed were more of the little people marching across my body.

I was so surprised that I cried out. My voice scared them, and they all ran off. Though it really hurt, I managed to pull my right arm free of the strings. With a tug of my head, I was able to loosen some of the pegs that held my hair to the ground. As soon as I could move my head a bit, I saw the little men coming back. There was a small army of them. They had their bows and arrows ready, aimed at me. They began to shoot.

It felt like a hundred needles were sticking into my left hand. They fired again, this time into the air. The tiny arrows landed all over me, like a painful rain. Through all this, I could hear the tiny men shouting in their little, shrill voices. I couldn't understand a word. What I heard sounded like: *Hekinah Degul,* whatever that meant.

The pain from the tiny arrows was bad. But I soon realized the darts did me little real harm. I saw some

of the little people run up with spears and try to stab me in the side. I was wearing a leather jacket. The spears couldn't get through. I recall thinking that although these little fellows were small, they did not lack for bravery.

By now, with one hand free, I knew I could free myself. Knowing these people could not really harm me, I took a moment to think. Once I freed myself and was on my feet, these tiny soldiers were no match for me. I made up my mind that if they shot any more arrows at me, I would harm them—small though they were.

It didn't come to that. When they saw I was staying still, a large group of them drew near me. I began to hear pounding noises coming from the other side of my head, right near my ear. It pulled my hair, but I was able to turn and see what was going on. The little people had built a flat wagon, right alongside me. They must have started putting it together while I had been asleep. The wagon was almost finished.

There was one little fellow who seemed to be in charge of the work. From time to time, he would give a long speech. The crowd of workmen would say something back and then go back to their work, even faster. I couldn't understand a word the little man in charge was saying. Whatever it was, it worked.

As the small people saw I was no longer struggling, they went to work with a will.[2] By this time, I was getting very hungry. I made motions with my free hand, pointing to my mouth. I pretended to eat imaginary food. They got the message. Ladders were set up alongside my face, and the soldiers began to climb them.

---

2. with a will with a strong purpose

On their tiny shoulders, the soldiers carried baskets of meat and bread. I had to smile. The loaves of bread were the size of small bullets. The meat might have been mutton. I couldn't tell by the taste. The whole animal they came from had to have been smaller than a mouse! I ate all the food, several baskets at a time. It took a while, but soon my stomach was full. They also brought me a number of barrels of pleasant-tasting wine to drink. Each barrel held no more than an ounce. It wasn't until a half hour later that I began to feel sleepy. As the darkness grew around me, I realized that the little people had drugged the wine! I passed out.

While I slept, the little people were busy. The machines that I saw had been put to good use. I had been hoisted onto the flat wagon I had seen beside me. I had then been tied down again.

I awoke in some sort of building. This time, I was firmly tied with small, but unbreakable, chains. The question was: Where was I?

I soon found out that I was in Mildendo, the capital city of the land of Lilliput. Fifteen hundred horses— each 4 1/2 inches high—pulled my wagon. I found this out when I was paid a visit by the emperor of Lilliput himself. Later, I found out why the building I was chained in was available. A terrible murder had happened there, and no one wanted to be in it. It also gave me some idea of what the Lilliputians thought of *me!*

I had to smile when the emperor showed up. A whole party of nobles and politicians entered before him. An important-looking follower made an announcement in their language. Then, with all the dignity[3] of a full-size king, Golbasto Momaren

---

3. dignity sense of self-importance

Evlame Gurdilo Shefin Mully Ully Gue, the emperor, made his entrance. His name and title were longer than he was!

If it were not for the small army of archers, with their needle-like arrows, I would have laughed out loud. But from the way he carried himself, I don't think the little monarch[4] had a sense of humor.

He looked me over as if I were some kind of rare animal that his army had captured and caged. He made a long speech. Then several of his followers talked to me in the same language. I caught a word here and there that sounded familiar, but that was it. In college, I had studied languages, and I speak no less than five. Little by little, I began to figure out what they were saying.

The emperor had ordered his best scientists to study me—the "strange animal." Others were put in charge of teaching me the Lilliputian language. The emperor appeared to be such a tiny man with such a big opinion of himself that I couldn't help laughing out loud. He was not amused. He barked an order, and the little archers shot a flight of arrows directly at me!

I had come to the end of my patience. I was chained, but I could move a little. I grabbed a handful of the little soldiers. I know I could have crushed them or thrown them to the ground. Somehow, even though they had shot arrows at me, I didn't. Instead, I played a trick. As the emperor watched in horror, I pretended to eat the little archers.

There was panic. What was left of the soldiers formed a ring around the little emperor. They were ready to lay down their lives to protect him. At this point, I couldn't help but admire their bravery. I

---

4. **monarch** king

laughed again and opened my hands, showing them the soldiers I had pretended to eat. I set them down gently on the ground. The little emperor saw they were unhurt.

The tiny monarch gave a series of commands to his company of followers. Then, still full of dignity, he left. This time, I didn't laugh. Moments later, I found out what the emperor had said. Because I could have killed his men but didn't, I had won my freedom. The chains would come off. If I continued to behave, there was a chance I could leave the building.

The Lilliputians weren't taking that many chances. While I had been drugged, they had taken my sword and my pistol. I didn't care for that. However, I could also understand it. What I really missed were my eyeglasses.

2 Capturing Blefuscu's Navy

For the next weeks, I began to learn the Lilliputian language. It wasn't that difficult, with my background in foreign languages. In very little time, I was able to have conversations with my teachers and began to learn about this land of small people. It wasn't too much later that I was invited to the royal court of Lilliput for an evening's entertainment.

I have read books about what goes on in the royal courts of foreign lands. Every Englishman knows what goes on in London's royal court. But I was in no way ready for what went on in the royal court of Lilliput. In a strange way, their entertainments made sense. Take the way that their politicians got their jobs, for example.

A thick rope—I would have called it a string—was stretched out between two posts, about two Lilliputian "feet" above the floor. To get their jobs, politicians had to dance on the rope. The longer they stayed on the rope, the longer the politicians stayed in office. I watched with great amusement as the tiny men did their best to stay on the rope.

A fellow named Flimnap was the best at doing this trick. His job was lord high treasurer. He was in charge of all the emperor's money. How he could dance on that rope! One of my teachers informed me that Flimnap had fallen once but had landed safely on a pillow. As I watched each politician try to dance and stay on the rope, I had a thought. How much more entertaining it would be if England had the same system instead of elections!

Then came the nobles.[1] To stay in favor with the emperor, they had to do a different trick. A stick was raised above the floor to a certain height. Each nobleman would pass under it. The next time, the stick was lowered. Finally, the stick was hardly off the floor at all. The nobleman who could lower himself most became the emperor's favorite. In that respect, Lilliput wasn't too different from England!

The rewards to the nobles for making themselves as low as possible were pieces of colored thread. They would put these threads on their jackets so that they could be plainly seen. It reminded me of the ribbons and medals that English nobles get from monarchs.

The emperor seemed to be having a good time. A group of Lilliputian soldiers were marched in to perform some fancy drills. I decided to join in the fun. "Your majesty's soldiers need a drill field," I said in my best Lilliputian.

I took out my pocket handkerchief and spread it on the floor. It made a perfect drill field for the tiny soldiers. As they went into their drill, I took the sides of my handkerchief and gently raised them into the air. The emperor was delighted by the sight. Then after the drills came the inspection of the troops. All the soldiers in the capital would march in review before the emperor.

I joined in again. This time, I stood with my legs apart and the tiny army marched between. The emperor was overjoyed at the sight. He rewarded me better than he did his politicians and nobles. I was to

---

1. **nobles** persons of royalty or high birth

be given my freedom—up to a point. I was given a parole, but there were conditions:

1. I could not leave Lilliput without permission. 2. I could not enter the capital without permission. 3. I would walk only on the roads, so as not to destroy crops or animals underfoot. 4. I would not handle or trample Lilliputians. 5. I would carry emergency messages for the emperor. This made sense, as I could walk faster than any of their tiny horsemen could ride. 6. I would fight against Lilliput's rival land, Blefuscu. 7. I would help out with any heavy-duty building work. 8. I would survey and measure the land of Lilliput.

In return for this, I would have food and drink enough for 1,728 Lilliputians. I am not sure how they arrived at that figure. I did learn, though, that these tiny folk were brilliant at mathematics. I swore to go by the emperor's rules. They seemed easy enough. But I noticed that the penalty for breaking the rules was death—and I still didn't have my sword or pistol!

Not long after, I began to look over the countryside. This odd land looked just like any other I had visited. It had towns, farms, hills, and streams. The only difference was that everything was about one-twelfth the size of regular human countries. I say this because I soon learned that Lilliput also had the same problems as regular nations. To the Lilliputians, their problems were just as big.

By the emperor's order, I was given a teacher who was to fill me in on his country's history and customs. The little chap's name was Reldresal. I had seen him at the palace. He was almost as good at rope dancing as was Flimnap. Reldresal gave me a tour of Lilliput's capital city, Mildendo.

He kept speaking of the city as a *metropolis*. I had learned not to laugh at the airs[2] these little people put on. But I couldn't help but smile at this "metropolis." The whole place wasn't more than 500 Lilliputian feet square. It seemed that the Lilliputians, despite their tiny size, liked to make themselves look bigger and more important to others.

As we toured the little city, Reldresal gave me some history of Lilliput. It had not always been so neat and orderly. The emperor had the final say in politics now. But at one time, there had been two political parties. The names in Lilliputian language are hard to pronounce. They wore different shoes. There was the high-heel party called Tramecksan and the low-heel party called the Slamecksan. It was that simple.

It seemed odd to me that this could make a difference. How much taller would high heels make a Lilliputian? But, as Reldresal talked, he mentioned Blefuscu. This caught my ear. It was part of my parole that I fight against Blefuscu. I was so happy to be free of chains and walk about that I hadn't asked about this duty.

Reldresal explained that years ago, a great religious argument arose in Lilliput. It even came to open battle. The emperor took one side and ordered the rebels to obey. Those who refused to obey were put to death. More than 11,000 Lilliputians had been killed. The rest of them fled to an island kingdom off the shores of Lilliput. This kingdom was called Blefuscu. The king of Blefuscu took the rebels in.

At this point, I had to interrupt Reldresal. I asked him just what this religious argument was about. I was amazed at his answer! The classic Lilliputian

---

2. **airs** showy attitude

breakfast was soft-boiled eggs. Some of the little people preferred to open their eggs at the big end. The others preferred the small end. My amazement turned to horror. Thousands had been killed over which end of the egg got opened!

I dared not say how foolish I thought this was. I knew that these little men were filled with dignity and airs about their doings. Reldresal went on. When the emperor of Lilliput demanded that Blefuscu return the "Big Enders," as they were called, the king of Blefuscu refused. Since that time, there had been war between the tiny countries. I kept as straight a face as I could. Reldresal was so serious about this foolishness.

It also seemed that because Blefuscu was an island, their little people were very good sailors. Lilliput had tried many times to invade Blefuscu and had failed each time. The navy of Blefuscu had fought off the Lilliputians. In fact, Lilliput had lost 40 ships so far.

Now, without a navy to defend itself, Lilliput was in danger of invasion by Blefuscu. Reldresal explained that this is where I came into the picture. I was going to be Lilliput's new secret weapon. What had I got myself into when I agreed to the parole?

Just how serious Reldresal and the emperor were about this war soon became apparent. Spies had discovered that the fleet of Blefuscu—some 50 ships— was ready to sail.

The Lilliputian military showed me their maps, but they were too tiny to read. I asked that my personal belongings be returned to me because I needed my eyeglasses. I was secretly hoping they would also give back my sword and pistol. But they gave me only what I needed—my glasses.

I saw that a narrow strip of water separated Blefuscu from Lilliput. I offered a plan to the

Lilliputian military leaders to take care of the enemy fleet. They were doubtful that my plan would work. They argued that the "sea" was too wild and dangerous.

I kept a straight face. To them, it may have been a sea. But the distance across the water was no more than a half mile. I knew my plan could work, and I finally got approval. The next morning at sunrise, I slipped into the chilly waters and began to swim toward Blefuscu.

None of the Blefuscudians knew of me. This was a great help. I supposed that if I were spotted, a lookout would think I was a small-size whale! I swam the last few yards underwater. I quickly snapped the anchor cables on all 50 ships. I broke to the surface and was immediately spotted. As I began to gather all of the ship's broken ropes together, a hail of arrows was shot at me.

When I had dealt with the armies of Lilliput, their arrows were painful but not harmful. My clothing stopped most of them. But in the water, these darts were aimed at my face and shoulders. Then I had an idea. With my free hand, I put on my eyeglasses and only blinked as the tiny arrows bounced off!

I gathered up all the cables and began to swim for the shores of Lilliput. This was too much for even the brave sailors of Blefuscu. They began to jump off the captive ships and swim for home. So it was that I returned to Lilliput with the entire fleet of Blefuscu in tow. What made me feel best was that not a single tiny life had been lost.

3 Lilliputian Laws

I became a national hero. The emperor gave me the title *Nardac*. Everywhere I went, the Lilliputians hailed me. I could say that they all looked up to me, but in view of my size, they would do that, anyway.

I enjoyed a great deal of freedom now. I could wander around so long as I kept the rules of my parole. It also gave me a chance to learn more about the society of these little people. What I did not really understand, the faithful Reldresal would explain.

What I found most interesting was what Reldresal told me about Lilliputian law. The worst thing a small person could do was to betray his country. Treason was punished by death. I could understand this easily. Most countries have the same law.

More unusual was how the Lilliputians treated accusers. If one tiny fellow says another has done a crime, there is a trial. If the fellow is innocent in England, he is simply let go. Nothing happens to the accuser.

In Lilliput, it is different. The one who accused falsely is then put to death! The man who is proved innocent is given a large cash reward.

I thought of how many times in my country men were falsely accused. To prove themselves innocent, they often spent all they had. Their lives were ruined. How different it would be in England if we had such laws. The number of false accusers would be tiny.

To swindle[1] someone out of his money is fraud.[2] This is punished in Lilliput by death. I had often thought this would be fair. How many lives have been ruined by fraud? But little happens to the one who commits it.

Strangest of all was Lilliput's law about ungrateful persons. Not to be grateful for a good deed done is a shameful thing in England or in any civilized country. But in Lilliput, lack of gratitude is punished by death!

It seemed that most of the Lilliputian laws were based on conduct. They were moral laws.[3] I sometimes feel that in my own country, people feel that the crime is not important. Not getting caught for the crime is the real goal.

Fraud is common in England's government. In Lilliputian government, however, there is no chance for fraud. Instead, only good, clever, moral men reach high office. There are no elections. There is no chance to lie in order to get a high office.

At this point, I had to interrupt Reldresal. How about the rope dance I saw at the palace? I had been told this is how a man reached office in Lilliput. Reldresal looked around him before he answered. It seemed he was afraid that someone might be listening.

He explained. There were many good laws in Lilliput. The bad laws were new ones. The country was ruled by an emperor. What an emperor said was law. The emperors before Golbasto Momaren had been wise, kind, and just. Golbasto Momaren was a different sort of man.

---

1. **swindle** cheat
2. **fraud** trickery; deceit
3. **moral laws** laws governing right or wrong behavior

It was the new emperor who started the rope dance. It was his idea for the nobles to make themselves low before him. The whole business of which end of the egg to open? That, too, was the idea of Golbasto Momaren.

I understood now why Reldresal had looked around before he answered. To disagree with an emperor is treason. The little fellow could have been put to death for what he had said to me. My admiration for Reldresal grew in that moment. He had risked his life to speak the truth.

He quickly changed the subject. I did not blame him. We spoke of Lilliputian family life. He said that the little folk do not marry because they want to have children. They marry because they are attracted to each other.

They don't feel that they owe anything to their children. Once a child is old enough, it is put in a boarding school. The parents must pay for each child in school. The parents live their own lives. This is the law. To hear Reldresal speak of it, the system worked well.

Reldresal said that the schools for noble children were different. There are separate schools for boys and girls. The schools are not fancy at all. Students are trained in honor and love of country. They have many classes in religion and courage. They are taught to be modest and to respect justice.

Parents are allowed to see the children only twice a year. These visits last exactly one hour each. I smiled. In my country, there are many children in boarding schools who never do see their parents.

What of the schools for the ordinary folk? Reldresal said they were almost the same as for nobles. The difference was that they didn't last as long as the schools for noble children. Workers and farmers had no schools at all for their children. As soon as a child was old enough to work, his life as a farmer or worker began.

What of the girls? I asked. Reldresal told me that Lilliputian women are trained to be neat and clean. They are taught to be nice to men always. They are all taught how to read. But they are not given the same books as boys. When I asked why, Reldresal smiled. It would only confuse them, he told me.

My talk with Reldresal was interrupted by a servant. We had both been invited to have dinner with the emperor. After the servant left, I questioned Reldresal. Was this a usual thing? He told me it was not. Further, he felt that something was going on.

4 My Enemies Tell Lies

Reldresal was right. Dinner with Golbasto Momaren was no fun. I had hoped the emperor had invited me to be praised for my good work. But I wasn't everyone's favorite person. True, I had stopped the invasion from Blefuscu. But the nobleman in charge of Lilliput's navy, Skyresh Bolgolam, became my enemy. After all, I had succeeded where he had failed.

Flimnap, too, joined with him in disliking me. Though he could dance on the rope better than any other, *I* had become the country's number-one hero. It became clear to me that just like their dignity and airs, the men of Lilliput could have human-size jealousy.

The two nobles began to tell lies about me to the emperor. Flimnap said that I cost too much to feed and keep. Now that Blefuscu was not a threat, he asked why I was needed. He showed the emperor lists of how much I ate.

He made another charge that was really silly. Flimnap said that his wife was crazy about me. He said that she was coming to see me secretly. The idea of a romance with a woman six inches tall was silly. But it seemed the emperor was listening.

They also said I had been too soft on the Blefuscudians. They felt I should have killed them instead of letting them escape. You might think that ending an invasion with no loss of life was a good thing. Certainly, I did.

But Bolgolam and Flimnap still had the emperor's ear. They were preparing the treaty to end the war with Blefuscu. They felt not enough had been done to that little island country.

I was to cross the waters again. This time, I was to destroy their cities and kill as many of them as I could! I argued that Blefuscu was no longer a threat. It had no navy and could no longer attack us. The argument might have gone on longer. But suddenly, there was a cry of "Fire!"

A section of the royal palace was in flames when I arrived on the scene. A string of Lilliputians were trying in vain to put out the flames with thimble-size buckets. I saw immediately that the fire was now too large for me to smother with my hands. But the long hours of talking with the nobles and drinking tiny barrels of wine gave me an idea.

Calling on the tiny firemen to stand back, I opened my britches and emptied my bladder on the blaze. In a short time and amid clouds of foul-smelling smoke, the fire went out. A great cheer rose from the little people. I expected that the emperor and his nobles would again hail me as a hero. Then I saw their faces. What was wrong?

My friend Reldresal quickly filled me in. I had, indeed, saved the royal palace. But the way in which I did it showed a lack of respect, my advisor told me. More and more, I was losing patience with the nobles and royal court of Lilliput. Hadn't I saved lives? The nobles would rather have seen people dead.

When the treaty talks began again, so did the lies my enemies told. Finally, I asked the emperor for permission to visit Blefuscu. I argued that few of their people had ever seen me. Once they saw my size and what I could do, they would be frightened to death.

They would do anything Lilliput wanted, and there would be no need to destroy their cities.

The emperor was still shocked and unhappy about my firefighting style. However, he agreed that my plan might work. He forgave me my "crime" in saving the palace. He also gave his permission for me to go to Blefuscu. I bowed and started to leave his royal court. As I did, I noticed Flimnap and Bolgolam already whispering in the emperor's ear. What lies were they telling now? I also did not miss the rather cold look on the emperor's face as he watched me leave.

I spent the next few days preparing for my visit to Blefuscu. I met with Blefuscu's ambassadors. All seemed to be going well. If my plan succeeded, lives would be spared, and there would be peace after many years. I must confess that I was feeling quite good about matters.

Then I heard from my friend Reldresal. I was about to be arrested for treason. It came as no surprise that Flimnap and Bolgolam had prepared a set of charges. I was guilty of treason for the way I had put out the fire and for talking to the Blefuscudian ambassadors. I was also accused of plotting to overthrow the emperor.

I almost laughed. "It will all come out at the trial," I said. Hadn't I ended the war? Hadn't I saved the palace from flames? You can understand my shock at what Reldresal told me: There was to be no trial. The emperor had accepted Flimnap and Bolgolam's charges. The penalty was death! I was outraged—after all I had done for these people!

Reldresal went on. The emperor was aware I had done great service to the crown. For that reason, I was not to be burned alive. Further, I would not have my food poisoned or be shot with poisoned arrows. I sighed a bit in relief. Then Reldresal delivered the next bit of news. In all his mercy, the emperor had decided that I would only have my eyes put out. Then, once I was blind and helpless, I would be starved to death!

I did what any sane man would do: I fled Lilliput. In the dark of night, I slipped to the water's edge with my belongings. I cut loose a Lilliputian war ship to carry them on. I then swam straight to Blefuscu. I reached their shores by sunrise and was greeted with cheers. These little people realized what I could have done to them, but refused to do. Here, at last, were grateful people!

The celebration didn't last long. In a few days, a Lilliputian war ship arrived. The word came down from the Lilliputian emperor. I was to be returned, or the war would begin again. This time, with no navy, Blefuscu had little chance. The people of Blefuscu didn't want to give me up, but what could they do? What's more, what could *I* do?

The next few days, I wandered alone along the shores of Blefuscu. There was no way that I would return to Lilliput and be blinded and starved. If I joined in a war against Lilliput, what would be the end result? I would be killing little people. That was why I had refused to kill Blefuscudians. Either choice was terrible.

I was sitting on a rock, looking out to sea, when I thought I saw something in the waters. I tore off my outer clothes and dove into the surf. In minutes I had reached it. It was a full, human-size boat! It appeared to be the very same small boat I had tried to launch when the *Antelope* had sunk! It was turned over in the water and in bad shape. Somehow, I got it back to shore.

I said nothing of this discovery. I returned to the

capital city of Blefuscu and told the king I was thinking about the emperor of Liliput's ultimatum.[1] It
bought me time. I worked day and night on the boat.
In a week, I had it ready for sea. It was only then that
I revealed my plan to the people of Blefuscu. For them,
it was an answer to a prayer. They could keep their
"honor" in Lilliput's eyes: I, the source of their problem
would be gone.

The good people of Blefuscu helped me out. They
gave me all sorts of food and drink for supplies. They
even gave me live animals for meat, in case I would be
at sea long. But the meat and other food would not
keep for long. So it was that on September 24, 1701, I
left the shores of Blefuscu.

I had learned much. I knew now that little people
can have evil within them that is much larger than
their bodies. I had learned, too, that there are good
and bad among all men, regardless of their size. I had
seen bravery and devotion to one's country. I had seen
lies and treachery in the name of that devotion. I also
hoped that I had seen the last of all folk six inches tall.

I had been prepared for a long time at sea. When
the *Antelope* sank, the nearest land had been
Australia. You cannot imagine my joy when, two days
out, I spotted a sail on the horizon. Amazing as it
sounds, the ship was English and bound for home! I
was taken aboard and gratefully greeted the ship's
captain. I explained that I had been on the *Antelope* as
the ship's doctor. To my knowledge, I was its only
survivor.

The captain knew of the loss of the *Antelope*. But he
couldn't believe I had survived all that time in a small
boat. I then told him the entire story. When I was

---

1. ultimatum final demand

done, he told me how sorry he was. He would have to have me locked up in chains. When I asked why, he explained. I could be a danger to myself and his crew. I was obviously crazy!

I could well have returned to England a prisoner and been sent to a madhouse. But then I remembered. I reached inside my pocket and set three tiny sheep and a Lilliputian cow on the captain's table. That proved my story better than any words. Not only did the captain believe me, but also he was excited about my "good fortune."

I laughed. I asked him what good fortune could that be? I had lost my ship. I had lost all my medical supplies, even my sword and pistol. With the *Antelope* gone, there was no one to pay me what I was owed. I would arrive in England penniless.

The captain told me I was wrong. I had the tiny animals. People all over England would pay to see such wonders. He assured me I would be a rich man within a year. I must confess that the captain was right. In a short time, my wife and I became wealthy. I had more than enough money to start a new medical practice. As long as the wee animals lived, more money would come.

But few things last forever. In a few months, I once again found myself at sea. But that is another tale, for another time. . . .

PART TWO:
A VOYAGE TO BROBDINGNAG

1 *In a Land of Giants*

Because it is not my nature to be still for long, once again I went to sea. Two months after my return from Lilliput, I sailed for the land of Surat, on board the ship the *Adventure*. She was a good ship and her captain, John Nicholas, was a good commander.

To reach Surat, we sailed down the coast of Africa. When we reached the Cape of Good Hope, it was storm season. We had to spend the winter there. In the spring, with plenty of food and water, we set sail. All seemed well at first. The weather was fair, and the winds moved us well. Then from nowhere, a dreadful storm came up.

We were blown far off our course. All we knew was we were somewhere in the North Pacific Ocean. We might well have made it back on course, but the worst happened. We were hit by the most feared of storms: a monsoon.[1] We were soon hopelessly lost. To make things worse, we had run low on water and food. We needed to find land.

Not long after, we came upon an island. It was not on Captain Nicholas's charts. We put a rowboat over the side. I and several crew members were to scout the island for possible food and, especially, water. The party split up so we could cover more ground. I was alone. I had never seen such tall trees and high grass before. Once in a while, a strange-looking bird would

---

1. **monsoon** a strong wind, occurring especially in the Indian Ocean

fly by. I had found no water, and so I headed back to the shore.

When I got there, my eyes grew wide. The boat was already in the water, and the other crew members were rowing for their lives. Hot behind them was a giant, easily 60 feet high! It seemed that the giant could not swim. The boat got away. However, once it reached the *Adventure,* I saw them raise the anchor. They set sail. I was alone. To my horror, the giant was wading back to shore—toward me!

I ran to find a hiding place. I returned to the field of grass that was as tall as trees. It grew close together and I felt I would be hard to spot. Tired from the running, I lay down to rest. A loud noise wakened me. The tree-size grass was falling all around me. I looked up and soon saw what was happening. The month was June; I knew that. The huge grass was giant wheat, and a crew of giants was cutting it down for harvest.

I don't know what would have happened if a falling wheat stalk had hit me. But luck saved me. One of the farm hands spotted me. Before I could run, he scooped me up in one huge hand. He brought me to the man in charge to show what he had found. The huge man turned out to be the owner of this giant farm. I could not understand what they said. Even if I had, their voices were so loud that I could not make out their words.

The farmer brought me to his house. He seemed amused by my size. Though he was huge, he treated me gently. He placed me inside his jacket pocket. I heard a female voice. The giant reached in his pocket and took me out. He set me on a table the size of a parade ground. I found myself looking at a woman who was tall as a church steeple. Beside her was a young girl. I could never call her little.

The farmer's wife didn't think I was cute. She reached over and picked me up by one leg. I think she was afraid I might bite. She held me up in front of her face to look closer. From that point of view, her skin looked like a plowed field. It was multicolored and had ugly patches. I suppose that my skin would have looked the same to anyone from Lilliput.

The big woman set me down on the table as she would an animal. She put me on all fours. I quickly stood up. That surprised her. I walked around a bit to show her I was no animal. The little girl, however, seemed delighted with me. In a voice as loud as thunder, she asked something of her parents. They spoke for some time until my ears hurt. It soon became clear what the girl had asked, as she picked me up and carried me to her room.

She reached into a monster doll crib and took out a doll. She tossed it into a corner. It landed like a falling tree. She then placed me in the doll's crib. She bent over me and made cooing noises. I had been given to the giant girl as a toy! I seemed to be no longer in danger. Yet, I was little more than a freak or a pet for a child.

As small children do, she soon left me alone. I stood up in the giant crib, looking for a way to escape. In the back of my mind, I thought of going back to the shore. There was always a chance that the *Adventure* might return for me. But it had to be several miles back to shore. I was thinking about what to do when I heard a strange noise. I turned and saw two rats the size of sheep. They were coming at me!

A normal-size rat is a dangerous creature. To see one this size was horrible. As they came at me, I drew my sword and pistol. The first rat charged. At the last second, I fired my gun. The ball struck the ugly monster between the eyes. It fell dead at my feet. Before I could think, the other was upon me. I cut at it with my blade, as I dodged its teeth and claws. I saw my chance. When it turned again, I pierced the filthy thing through its heart. I was badly shaken, but unharmed.

The dying screams of the rats brought the family on the run. It also brought the family cat. The creature was the size of a tiger. As the family watched, the cat grabbed both rats from the crib. It set them on the floor and began to eat them. The sound of bones crunching gave me shivers. I felt lucky the cat didn't think of *me* as a meal.

But my courage changed the way that the farmer's wife looked at me. I was no longer a freak. I was a tiny hero. She gave me food and drink. But she still didn't think of me as human. I found that out after she fed me. She put me outside the house. I realized she expected me to go to the bathroom out there, as a dog or a cat would.

I thought for a moment. If I did that, she would always think of me as an animal. But the size of the giants' bathroom wouldn't allow me to use it. With a shrug, I relieved myself. The giant woman and her daughter watched. I don't know if it was out of curiosity. Maybe they wanted to make sure I didn't run away. When I was done, the little girl picked me up. Both she and the woman kept saying the same words to me. I had the sinking feeling that they meant: "Good boy!"

2 I Become a Performer

My life as a plaything for the giant girl was not unpleasant. As children do, she spoke to me endlessly. In a short time, I began to understand their language. The name of this land was Brobdingnag. The giant girl's name was Glumdalclitch. She named me Grildrig. I also learned why I was at first called Splacknuck.

There is an animal of that name native to Brobdingnag. It is about six feet long and somewhat resembles a human. At first, the huge people thought I was a new kind of splacknuck. But after a time, I managed to convince Glumdalclitch I was not. As to the farmer and his wife, I was never quite sure what they thought I was.

One evening, a friend of the farmer came to visit. Naturally, I was called on to perform. I had quickly learned what amused the big people. They enjoyed seeing me behave in a perfectly normal human way. This may not sound funny. However, if a normal human had an animal who behaved human, it would be considered amusing. It was like watching a trained monkey to them.

The farmer's friend began to talk excitedly. He felt a great deal of money could be made. I would be shown to the townspeople as a trained splacknuck. The farmer's friend felt that people would pay to see me perform. The farmer agreed, and plans were made. Naturally, no one asked me about this. After all, I was the property of the farmer.

I found myself in an odd position. It was not too different from being put outside after meals to relieve myself. I could insist I was not an animal. But if I did, I was no longer something people would pay to see.

With the farmer, I had a safe place, food, and shelter. I also had a loving friend in Glumdalclitch. To be on my own in a land of giants was frightening and dangerous. So it was that I became a trained, performing splacknuck!

We were a hit from the very start. All the people in our small town showed up at the marketplace. They paid to watch me perform. I went through the motions of sword fighting. I tossed a spear. The people even clapped when I would eat and drink from Glumdalclitch's doll dishes. In short, all I had to do was act human. The people never tired of seeing me do this. No splacknuck had ever done such things.

We kept moving from town to town. By now, the farmer was making a good deal of money. The towns where I performed got bigger and bigger. I heard the farmer discussing a trip to Lorbrulgrud. I knew not where that was. The farmer kept calling it "the pride of the universe." With careful listening, I found out. Lorbrulgrud was the biggest city in all of Brobdingnag. We were headed for the big time!

Lorbrulgrud may have been a big city, but the people were the same. They never became tired of seeing me perform. But I was becoming tired. I did so many shows each day that my health was failing. I fell sick. The farmer did not understand this. He made me keep doing shows.

In England, I had often seen performing animal shows. At times, when an animal wouldn't do its tricks, a trainer would use a whip. I thought nothing of this at the time. The thought never came to me what happened to these animals. I believe it was the custom to destroy them when they could no longer perform. Sometimes, they may have died from being over-worked. I now found myself in that sorry state.

I'm sure the farmer did not mean to be cruel. For all their size, the Brobdingnagians were gentle folk. Surely, there could be no sweeter and kinder person than my Glumdalclitch. But I was not a small human to the farmer. I was a only a different sort of splack-nuck. In my illness, I might have died. But the luck that has saved my life so many times again came to my rescue.

There had been much talk about me in the big city. After a time, it reached the queen. We had been called to Flanflasnic, where the royal palace is located. I was to give a command performance for the queen. Knowing this and seeing how badly I was feeling, the farmer allowed me a day's rest while we traveled to the royal city.

I was still nearly spent.[1] I somehow got through a whole show for the queen at the palace. At the very end, as I bowed to the giant queen, I passed out. In a daze, I felt gentle giant hands pick me up. I do not know for how long I slept.

When I awoke, I thought all had been a dream. Surely I was back in England. But I was in a wonder-fully rich bedroom. My covers were of the finest cloth. There were paintings on the walls, and the furniture was of the finest quality. My bed was so elegant that it could have been a work of art. The "dream" soon came to an end. Through my bedroom window, I saw a giant eye peeking in.

I soon found out what had happened. After I had

---

1. **spent** very tired; exhausted

passed out, the queen had bought me from the farmer. This amazing bedroom was really in a doll's house made for the queen. That's why it was so luxurious. I may have been sold like any other performing animal, it is true. But I was now living in a place richer and finer than any I had ever known. It was the equal of any to be found in London itself.

The huge eye had belonged to a servant. At least, that is what I thought at the time. I later found out who was the owner of that eye. I also was at risk of my life from its owner!

3 Learning About Size

Later, I was awakened again by a familiar voice. The ceiling of my bedroom swung open on a hinge. I looked up into the face of my dear Glumdalclitch. It was she who explained what had happened.

The queen had been crazy about me. I was like a new toy to her. When I had passed out, she was very concerned. She ordered that this special bedroom be made for me. The finest workmen in Brobdingnag had built the room.

My clothing had been made by the royal doll maker. The paintings on my walls were miniatures by the best artists. Some of the furniture had been made by carpenters.

The queen had been impressed by the way Glumdalclitch had acted when I passed out. She saw how much the giant girl cared about me. She ordered that Glumdalclitch was to be my personal nurse and guardian. The huge girl had been caring for me during my illness.

She had changed my bedclothes and even my outer wear. I would have been embarrassed, had I not been so ill. Then I thought about another thing. This girl had made sure I relieved myself outdoors each night. There was little she had not already seen.

When it was known that I had recovered my health, food and drink were brought. I ate off the finest doll's dishes. I drank from the best cups. I found that new clothes had been made for me while I slept. I put them on and gazed into a mirror. To a

Brobdingnagian, I was dressed as finely as any noble.

Soon, I was brought before the queen. I think she thought of me as a new toy. She brought me before the king. She seemed surprised at what the king did.

The great man thought I was not a splacknuck, but the result of some evil spell. He called in all the wise men of the kingdom to look me over. Finally, I thought, I could speak with educated men. I was a doctor; surely, I could explain to them what I really was. It was almost a waste of time.

These men cared more about what others thought. They spoke to each other in strange terms they made up to show how wise they were. As for my talking, they dismissed it. They thought my words were like those a parrot speaks. They felt I had no idea what I was talking about. But in the end, they decided I was not the result of an evil spell. I was only a freak of nature—a different sort of splacknuck.

The king felt better about their news. To the people of Brobdingnag, I was still a strange animal. The king even invited me to dinner. A special chair and table were prepared for me. They were set atop the king's table, between him and the queen.

I watched these huge people eat. By turns, I was interested and disgusted. It must have been because of their size. The queen was a delicate eater. She had a plate of roasted larks before her. In England, these birds are no bigger than a few inches. Their bones are so small that they are eaten whole.

In Brobdingnag, larks are the size of turkeys. The queen ate them whole. To her, they were delicate. From where I sat, I could hear the bones crunch between her teeth. It gave me chills. The king was a hearty eater. He had great slabs of beef and mutton before him. The sounds could turn a man's stomach.

After dinner, the king started a conversation. He was curious. I had said I was from England. He wanted to know what a land full of splacknucks was like. This was my chance. I would tell him about my country. I would speak of England's glory.

I told the king how English government worked. I spoke of the royal family and their nobles. He seemed interested. From time to time, he would nod his head. Other times, he smiled.

I told him about English law. I spoke of how our money system worked. I must say that I was truthful in all details. I am not proud of many things in England. I told him of the rich and poor. I told him about how politicians can lie to get elected. I tried to leave out nothing.

I wasn't sure what to expect when I finished. The king threw back his head and roared with laughter. I asked politely what was so funny. He found it hard to answer. He kept breaking up with laughter. He wiped his eyes with a napkin the size of a large blanket and began to speak.

The idea of a whole land of tiny people amused him. He called our houses and places burrows—holes in the ground. The idea of an animal six inches tall acting like a man was hilarious. How could there be a king upon whom Brobdingnagians could step like an ant? How could there be an army of splacknucks whom a horse could squash under its hoofs? To the huge king, our cannons would be pea shooters. Every time I tried to explain, it became worse. It only made him laugh harder.

I was terribly embarrassed. I said no more. The king said that if he ever needed a good laugh, I could

tell him more about England. I didn't show how I felt. After all, he *was* the king.

Then I thought about my stay in Lilliput. I had found the airs of Golbasto Momaren just as funny. I had stolen an entire fleet of ships from Blefuscu. Their armies and navies were but toys to me. I recalled how I had laughed when I put out the fire at the palace in Lilliput.

The only tiny person I had respected was Reldresal. Now I had learned something. People may be small in size but their ideas and their honor can be as large as a giant's. Now, being considered an animal, I was denied honor and respect. It was not a good feeling.

4 The Bird Carrier

However, being the queen's pet, I did not lead a bad life. She took me everywhere she went. At odd times, she would take me out and play with me. I began to grow fond of the giant lady. She was a sort of grown-up Glumdalclitch.

But I was not everyone's favorite. All through dinner, I was aware of something. There was a figure in the shadows. When the king and queen left, I saw him clearly. I was waiting for Glumdalclitch to come and get me. The figure moved toward the table.

It was a dwarf. But in Brobdingnag, a dwarf is 25 feet tall! In many countries, the royal family will keep a dwarf. They are amused by its size. These dwarfs are often quite clever. They do tricks. They tell jokes. They are often favorites of the king or queen.

This "little" fellow did not seem jolly. As he drew near, I recognized his eyes. It was the dwarf who had peeked into my bedroom when I was sick. An uneasy feeling came over me.

This dwarf had been the queen's favorite. He had been a sort of pet, like I was now. But I had taken his place. He was not happy about this. Before I knew it, the dwarf had grabbed me. I had been at a royal dinner, so I wore no sword. It would have been of little use against this giant dwarf.

He jumped up on a giant chair with me in his fist. He was where the king had sat. The remains of the dinner were still on the table. Among them was a giant hambone. To my horror, the dwarf stuffed me inside

41

the bone. With one filthy finger, he pushed me far inside. He then ran off.

What was I to do? In a few minutes, the servants would arrive. They would clear off the table. I could not be seen inside the hambone. I could be thrown out with the garbage. Worse yet, I could be thrown to a giant dog.

I thought of how the lark bones had crunched in the queen's mouth, and she was a dainty eater. What would some giant hound do to my tiny bones? A dog might not even notice that it was eating me. I was about to despair. Then I heard Glumdalclitch calling out my name: "Grilarig!"

I raised a great cry. I could only hope that she would hear me. I was lucky that Glumdalclitch was a child. To my ears, the voices of the Lilliputians had been high, tiny, and squeaky. So was mine in Brobdingnag. But children hear high-pitched noises better than grownups.

Glumdalclitch found me. I was dirty and greasy from the hambone. But I was not really hurt. I had many suits of fine clothes; there was no real harm done. However, it had been a close call. My giant nursemaid asked how it had happened.

I looked around. Off in the corner was the figure of the dwarf. I could tell the truth. If I did, the little fellow would surely be put to death. He could have killed me on the spot. Instead, he had hid me. All he wanted was the queen's love again. I could understand that.

I told Glumdalclitch that it had been an accident. I had been looking over the table and fell inside the bone. I had spared the dwarf's life. I hoped he would be grateful. In the future, I would be careful. I was lucky. I had no more problems with the dwarf.

Life went on at the giant palace. There was only one more dangerous thing that happened. It wasn't because of the dwarf. The rooms of the palace had no window screens. One day, I was attacked by giant wasps. The insects had smelled the remains of my meal. I looked through the window of my bedroom and saw a wasp the size of a turkey. It was trying to get in!

I ran and got my sword. The ugly creature had its head inside my window. I gave a mighty swing and cut off its head. It was soon followed by yet another giant insect. I used my sword again and again. Four dead wasps now lay at my feet.

Suddenly, a sound like thunder came. The room shook beneath my feet. Was it an earthquake? The shaking stopped. No more wasps came to my window. I looked outside. There was Glumdalclitch with a fly swatter. She had saved me again.

There were times when she could not help me. Glumdalclitch was, after all, a servant. When the queen or noble ladies were around, she was sent away. The queen never seemed to tire of me as a toy. I spent much of my time in her company.

A child buys clothes and tiny things for its dolls. The queen treated me the same way. She had learned that I was a sailor. This was fascinating to her. First, I did not know why, but I later found out that Brobdingnag had no navy.

One day, I was summoned to the royal garden. The queen and several noble ladies were there. The garden was huge. Each rose was over a yard wide. The thorns on the rose bushes would have made swords for a normal-size man.

In the center of the garden was what would have been a pond to the giants. To me, it was the size of a playing field. It was here that the queen showed me a surprise gift. She had had her workmen make a boat for me. They couldn't have known much about boats. It was not well made.

The queen insisted I get into the clumsy craft. I obeyed. I hoisted the crude sail. Then the noble ladies all began to wave their fans. The result was a gentle breeze to them. To me, in my toy boat, it was nearly a gale. The boat raced across the waters of the pond.

It took all my skill as a sailor to stay afloat. I was so busy that I did not see danger ahead. I ran into a waterlily pad in the center of the pond. It was like hitting the shore of an island. It did not sink my boat. For this I was grateful. But seated on the lily pad was a frog the size of a tiger!

The creature regarded me with one frightening yellow eye. I did not move a hair. Perhaps it had not seen me? Suddenly, yards of slimy tongue shot from its mouth. I moved quickly, and it missed me. I drew my sword.

The tongue came flying at me again. This time, I dodged and cut. Six feet of frog tongue lay at my feet. It still moved. I had not chased off the creature. It began to move toward me. I saw those great green claws. They could crush me in a second.

The frog was getting closer. Suddenly, there was huge explosion in the water. A great splash of water rose into the air. The lily pad and huge frog disappeared. Yet another explosion came. I struggled to keep my toy boat from tipping over.

I looked to shore and saw what had caused the giant splashes. My faithful nurse was there. She had picked up a handful of pebbles. She had thrown a few at the frog. What I thought were bombs falling about me were only pebbles. But they had done the trick.

I managed to get my boat back to shore. I expected that a fuss would be made over me. They would care about me. I knew the queen would care. I was wrong. The queen wasn't there.

When she had seen me sailing in the toy boat, she had been amused enough. She had gone off. That left me in the company of the noble ladies. They thought the whole business with the frog was terribly funny.

I was not amused, particularly when they sent Glumdalclitch away. They began to chatter and gossip. One of them decided to take a swim. I learned then that there are no bathing suits in Brobdingnag. In a few moments, all the giant women were naked before me.

In the past, I had found these giants to be modest folk. I was surprised that these women would undress in front of me. Then it sank in. Why shouldn't they? They would undress in front of a cat or a dog. To them, I was a splacknuck—an animal.

I suppose that they were attractive. But their size took away all pleasure from seeing them. Have you ever examined your own skin under a magnifying glass? It is not pretty to see. These "beautiful" ladies had skin like blotchy leather.

Their body hair was like a porcupine's quills. Their voices raised in laughter hurt my ears. They splashed each other. At the edge of the pond, the ripples were like tidal waves. I retreated as far as I could from the shoreline.

When my nurse returned to bring me to lunch, I was soaked. I was cold, and I must admit, frightened. I knew there was no bad intent on the part of the

noble ladies. They would never harm me on purpose.
But like a toy in the hands of a careless child, I could
be broken.

A few months later, there was excitement in the
royal court. The king and queen were going to make a
tour of the kingdom. The entire court would travel
with them. That also meant me. The queen had a special carrier made for me. It was the size of a royal living room. It had all the luxuries. It also had a large
handle on top so it could be picked up and carried by
a servant. I spent what should have been many
happy days in it. But no matter how good my life was,
it was not enough. I was still a prisoner. I was still
an animal.

I did not get to see a great deal of Brobdingnag, but
it was a most interesting place. The king himself told
me much about the land. It is about 6,000 miles long.
It is not an island at all, but part of Asia. The reason
that it does not appear on maps is simple.
Brobdingnag has no seaports, so no ships stop there.
To the north, there are huge volcanoes that separate it
from the rest of Asia.

This explains how such a strange place could not
be known to Europeans. It also explains how this land
is unique. There are no forces from outside to change
things. It is like a kingdom in Europe many, many
years ago.

There is only one major city—the capital. All the
rest is farmland and villages. Every one of these we
visited. The people turned out to cheer the king. They
also came to beg. Brobdingnag has no special treat-
ment for the poor or handicapped. Those who cannot
work must beg.

Most of the people of Brobdingnag were poor, and

many were beggars. They came in great numbers to see the king. It only made sense to beg from the rich, and the king was the richest man of all.

I could not believe the sorry state of these beggars. They were all deformed or diseased. They were covered with great open sores. Fleas the size of small birds crawled on their skin and in their clothes. Their cries for money nearly deafened me.

I have seen the poor of many countries. But in a way, I did not see them. Most people avoid looking at the poor. It makes then uneasy. This is even more true of the handicapped. People may throw money in a beggar's hat and walk on. They don't want to look closely.

But when a beggar is 60 feet high, he cannot be ignored. When his limbs are twisted, they are plain to see. An open sore a yard wide cannot be ignored. After a time, I stayed inside my carrier. I may have been a coward, but I could watch no more.

Other than the beggars, the giant people were interesting. Perhaps it was because Brobdingnag lies close to Asia. They were of all races and colors. Yet, this mattered not to them. If they had one thing in common, it was poverty.

I began to realize how well off the father of Glumdalclitch was. He had farmhands working for him. His house had separate rooms. His child was well dressed. Even so, in England he would have been a poor farmer.

I also realized why he had worked me so hard. The chance for a man of his station to make money was tiny. What he had made showing me would last him a lifetime. I had often thought of my debt to Glumdalclitch. She had nursed me. She had saved me from the plans of the dwarf. I knew now that her family had been repaid by my work.

I was also happy to find out that the queen liked Glumdalclitch. She now traveled everywhere with us. She was part of the royal court. For a poor farmer's daughter, this was a great thing. Had I not been found, she would have lived her life on the farm.

My own life was a good one. I could not deny that. Yet I was not free. I was not really a man. A cage made of gold is still a cage. I had searched for my fortune for years. Here in the land of giants, I had found it. I would have traded it all for my freedom. A humble ship's doctor was better than a royal pet.

Then one day, I heard some great news. The queen was taking a trip to the seashore. I would go with her, of course. I could not hide how happy I was. If I could get free near the ocean, I had a chance at freedom. The *Adventure* was long gone, but there could be other ships. Perhaps I could even make some crude sort of boat!

The day finally arrived. When the royal family arrived at the shore, I was given to the care of a servant. He brought me within sight of the ocean. What good was that? My carrier was locked. I could see the water through the closed windows of my carrier. But I could not get out. I was almost in tears.

The servant went off on an errand of some sort. I was alone at the shore. I tried the windows. It was no use. They were made for the giants to look in on me. They were not made to be opened. I was nearly mad with despair. Then I felt the strangest feeling. Someone or some thing had picked up my carrier. I ran from window to window and saw nothing outside. Then I realized I was in midair. Somehow, the carrier was flying!

While the servant was away, some great bird—perhaps a giant eagle—had picked up my carrier in its claws. I ran from window to window. The ground had disappeared. We were over the open sea. I could hear the beating of the great bird's wings above me. Once in a while, the creature let out a thundering cry. On and on we flew. I had no idea where we were going. Then, without reason, the bird released its grip. My carrier was falling . . . falling! With a great crash, I landed in the sea. I struck my head, and all was darkness.

I awoke to a feeling any sailor knows well. It was the gentle rolling of the sea. I looked about me. I was still inside the carrier. It had been well made. It did not let in the water. Half my dream had come true. I was away from Brobdingnag and far out at sea. But for all that, I was still a prisoner inside the cursed box!

I do not know how long I drifted. The food inside the box was eaten up. I was surrounded by all the luxuries that the queen's craftsmen had made for me. I had the finest of doll's clothes. I would have traded them all for an open boat and supplies. I was ready to give up. Then I heard a noise atop my carrier . . . and voices!

I nearly wept for joy. They were not the thundering tones of giants. The voices were those of normal men. Most wonderful of all, they were speaking English! I had been seen by a passing English ship. My carrier was being brought aboard. You can only imagine the surprise of the crew when it was opened and I stepped out: a free man on an English ship once more.

I was soon shown into the company of the captain. He name was Thomas Wilcocks. Just to hear a good

English name like that filled me with joy. It was not to last. I told him my story of the land of giants. At first, I thought he believed me. After a time, it became plain he thought I was insane.

This did not surprise me. The captain of the ship that had rescued me after Lilliput had thought me mad, too. Then I remembered how I had convinced that captain. We went up on deck, and Wilcocks inspected the inside of my carrier. He saw all the luxurious possessions that the queen's craftsmen had made for me. But it was the huge handle atop the carrier that convinced him. No human hand could ever be that size.

So it was that I was bound for home once more. I had lost all my possessions aboard the *Adventure*. But the ones I had from Brobdingnag were worth a fortune.

As we sailed for home, I thought of the giants and their land. For all their size, they were not dangerous. I had not been harmed by them. In fact, I had led a life of luxury. The giants were sweet, gentle folk at heart. It was as though someone had removed all the bad from their huge bodies.

I smiled to myself. Most of the little people of Lilliput had more evil in their tiny bodies. Most Lilliputians carried more airs and false dignity.

In a way, I thought, those little folk were not too different from my countrymen, the English. Then I put that thought from my mind. Surely, Englishmen could not be like that. Or could they? But what did it matter? I was wealthy. I was free. Best of all, I was on my way home!

PART THREE:
A VOYAGE TO LAPUTA

1 *The Floating Island*

It felt good to be back in England. But after a time, I felt the call; to the sea once more. I shipped out on the *Hopewell*, a trading ship bound for the Isle of Tonquin.[1] Once there, I boarded a sloop—a much smaller sailing craft. It was my idea to explore the islands around Tonquin. Many others had made their fortunes this way.

A terrible storm came up. My sloop was blown far from any shore. I was happy to spot a larger ship ten days later. To my horror, it was a pirate ship! I was taken prisoner. It was because I was a doctor that my life was spared. Had I been a trader or soldier, I would have been lost. The pirates put me over the side in a small canoe. I had little water and less food. At least I was alive.

I found a number of small islands as I drifted. None of them had plants to eat or water to drink. I was giving up hope when I saw yet another island. By now, I didn't care what it was like. It was solid land. I pulled the canoe ashore. The land was rocky, and few plants grew. I would search for food and water, I promised myself. But first, I needed rest on land.

Next morning, I walked on the beach. I noticed a strange cloud drifting toward me. I had never seen such a strange thing. As it came closer, my mouth dropped open in surprise. It was not a cloud at all. It was a great island that floated in the air!

---

1. **Isle of Tonquin** the gulf of Tonkin in the South China Sea

I waved my arms and cried out. Someone up above must have seen me. The island in the air stopped moving. In a few minutes, a chair, attached to ropes and wheels, was lowered. I suppose I was expected to get into it. I thought for a moment. What had I to lose? The land I was on seemed to offer me no shelter, water, or food. I got into the chair and was pulled high up into the air.

No one could have been prepared for what I saw when I stepped out of the odd chair. I was in the middle of a crowd of people. But what people! Their clothes fit them poorly. Their garments were covered with pictures of moons, suns, and planets. In between these pictures were notes of music. The strangest thing was these people's heads. Each head sloped either right or left. One eye looked that way, and the other looked straight up at the sky.

From the way they dressed, some were masters and others servants. Some of the servants carried short sticks with bladders blown up like balloons tied to the ends. Inside the balloons were either pebbles or peas. Whatever they were, they rattled. I was surprised to see the servants hit their masters in the head or mouth with the balloons. I later found out why.

These people spent most of their time thinking deep, deep thoughts. They became so lost in their thoughts that they hardly spoke or listened. It was the job of the servants to get their attention. To make their masters listen, they were hit on the ear. To make them speak, they were hit in the mouth. I learned that these servants were called Flappers.

No important person went anywhere without a Flapper. The most important person in the crowd around me had many Flappers. It turned out that he was the king of this island in the sky. It was my good

luck that the king loved meeting new and strange people. I was taken to the palace and given an apartment.
I was given a royal dinner. After that, I was greeted by
a person of importance. He had two Flappers.

It turned out that he was to be my teacher. The
king wanted to know all about me. To do that, I had to
learn his language. The teacher and I set to work. I
have mentioned my natural gift for learning languages. It took a month for me to be able to speak
their language. I also learned the history of this
strange land, *Laputa*. The name means "flying or float-
ing island."

I also learned how the island flew. It was in the
shape of a circle and about 10,000 acres in size.
The bottom was hard rock. In the middle of the
island, in the air, was a huge magnet. The island
would go up or down depending on how the Laputans
turned this magnet. Atop the island were regular
farms and towns.

I found out these things from my teacher, but it was
hard work. The Laputan men are all deep thinkers. If
not for the Flappers, nothing would get done. That was
why their clothes fit so badly and their houses were
crooked. No one could be bothered with small details.
After a time, I wondered how anything got done at all.

I asked my teacher how the Laputans moved the
island from place to place. He explained for so long
and in such complicated words that I fell asleep. When
I woke up, he was still explaining. I never did find out
how the island worked. But I did find out how the
Laputans had become as rich as they were.

Not far from where they found me was another
island. It was named Balnibarbi. The Laputans con-
trolled this other island from the air. Unless the people
of Balnibarbi did what they said, the Laputans would

drop huge rocks on them like bombs. The people below had no defense for these attacks from the air. The Laputans told the island people what they wanted. The goods and gold were put into big boxes and pulled up to Laputa on ropes.

As we got closer to Balnibarbi, I gave a lot of thought to the Laputans. Their lives and buildings were very sloppy. They didn't care. To them, it wasn't important. They got rich off others. This was not because they were so smart but just because their island could fly.

After a while, the king lost interest in me. He was thinking deep thoughts again. By using his Flapper, I got the king's attention. I told him I would like to explore Balnibarbi. He told me I could. He ordered a servant to give me a letter to the king of Balnibarbi. I would be treated like an honored guest. When I tried to thank the king of Laputa, it was too late. He was lost in thought again.

I was lowered by the same chair to Balnibarbi. I was given a royal welcome. The king of Laputa's letter saw to that. I had been shocked by the sloppy buildings and clothing of the Laputans. But it was nothing compared to what I saw here. It seemed that nothing worked right.

The Balnibarbians always had some big project going. Every last one turned out to be a failure. There was a mill that was supposed to grind grain for both Balnibarbi and Laputa. After years of work, the people of this island couldn't make it grind.

I asked the king how he could stand everything being so sloppy and wrong. He told me that all the plans for Balnibarbi came from Laputa. He added that everyone knew the Laputans had great minds. I then asked why they kept following bad plans. I was told that the Balnibarbians blamed themselves. Besides, he said, the people of this island had to do what Laputa said. Otherwise, they would be bombed.

I shook my head in wonder. Here were two countries that together could have had a fine life. The Balnibarbians weren't sloppy. They stayed awake. They worked hard. But the work they were given to do was too complicated. The Laputans cared only for ideas, not details. The Balnibarbians were fine on details, but short on ideas.

It was plain that they would never get together. I was told this had gone on for as long as anyone could remember. I was but a visitor. It was not my place to change them, even if I could. There was no point in staying any longer.

2 Calling Up the Past

In my conversations with the king of Balnibarbi, I heard of a wonderful land nearby. It was called Glubbdubdrib. It was not the odd name that caused my interest. The king told me that the island was ruled by a government of magicians. These men could call up any great figure from history! I could not resist the chance. I could talk with Julius Caesar, with the great poet, Homer. Anyone I chose could be summoned. With the king's help, I got a boat to Glubbdubdrib.

I was greeted there in a most friendly manner. I must say that it was a pleasant change from Laputa and Balnibarbi. Everything in this land worked right. The buildings were straight and clean. The people's clothing fit right. If anything went wrong, they repaired it by magic. Everyone I met seemed cordial. This was understandable. The wizards of Glubbdubdrib feared no one. Why should they, with their powers?

The governor of Glubbdubdrib told me about his special way of getting servants. He or any of the magicians could call up the dead and use them for servants. He could choose anyone. However, the spell was only good for 24 hours. He considered this a minor problem. For me, it was no problem at all. I only wished to speak with some famous figures of history.

I was given a place to live and good food and drink. I also got new clothes that fit properly. I settled in. I could now speak with famous people from history. The first persons I called up were Alexander the Great, Julius Caesar, and Hannibal. Who would not want to speak with the greatest generals of all time?

I was never so disappointed in my life. It is written in history that Alexander the Great died by poison before he finished conquering the world. It was not true. Fever carried him away. It was written that Hannibal opened a way through the Alps by destroying a great stone in his path. In fact, his army went around it.

Perhaps the saddest of all was Caesar and his killer, Brutus. I asked Caesar how it felt to have all that glory in history books. All he talked of was how much he was angry with Brutus. He kept saying that Brutus was only famous because he killed Caesar. Brutus claimed that he had saved Rome. They were still going at it when I sent them back.

One by one, I called up great philosophers and poets. Aristotle turned out to be a nasty, cranky old man. He refused to talk much with me. He felt it was a waste of his time. He had more serious things to think about. Thinking he might speak in the company of Homer, I called up that poet. Much has been written about their admiration for each other. The truth soon became plain. They had never met and didn't care to, either.

So it was with a handful of other philosophers and poets. Alas, they were not so great. They were only men, filled with the foolishness and small opinions of common men. Over a week's time, I came to this conclusion: Never believe what you read in history books. Perhaps the blame was not with these "great" men. It may be that those who write history made up lies. The lies were more interesting than the truth. I had no more to learn here. I made ready to leave Glubbdubdrib.

It was my intent next to visit the land of Luggnagg. This was not without danger. The Luggnaggians hated the English. I sailed for that land, posing as a Dutchman. For once, the trip was an easy one, with no storms. I was feeling good when I landed in the capital city. My joy was not to last.

The king of Luggnagg also hated the Dutch. As I waited my turn at the palace, I learned much. The king of Luggnagg was often moody. When he was unhappy, no one's life was safe. This was true even of those closest to him. This was shown in the way one had to approach the king.

As he sat on his throne, everyone had to approach on hands and knees. As they did this, they had to lick the floor as they crawled along. If the king was in a bad mood, he had poison put on the floor. When one of the politicians died of the poison, his body was taken away. Then servants would sweep the floor. I prayed that when my turn came, they had swept it well.

To my surprise it went well. The king had changed his mind about the English. Now it was only the Dutch he hated. When I told him where I really came from, all was well. I would be allowed free run of Luggnagg. I was given a place to stay as well.

While waiting for my audience with the king, I had heard some wonderful stories. There was a race of men in this land called Struldbruggs. They were supposed to be immortal! If I could find out their secret, my fortune would be made. Who would not want to live forever? I made arrangements to visit these men.

I had marvelous ideas about them. They would be wise with all they had learned in hundreds of years. They would be wealthy. They had had centuries to build their fortunes. They could advise me on how to use my own time better. My head was filled with visions of wealth, wisdom, and immortality.[1]

I had been disappointed by the "great" men of history. But this was nothing compared to what I learned now. Yes, the Struldbruggs lived forever. But they also grew older and older. They got weaker and weaker. Alas, they never got any wiser. I had always believed that experience would give a man great wisdom. All that it gave the Struldbruggs was great age.

When I returned to the capital of Luggnagg, I received happy news. There was a boat leaving for Japan. I knew that the emperor of Japan hated Christians. But I had papers saying that I was not a Christian. I also had an introduction to the emperor from no less than two kings. The king of Luggnagg also made me a gift of gold pieces and a red diamond. I later sold these in England for 1,100 pounds.

The best part was that from Japan, I could get a boat bound for home. Again, I had a peaceful voyage. As we sailed, I thought back on what had happened. I had not made my fortune. But I had learned much. I had learned from the Laputans that great knowledge does not always make a people great. I had learned from Balnibarbi that great plans do not always make for great results.

I had learned from Glubbdubdrib that history can be a pack of lies. Saddest of all, I learned from the Luggnagg people that great age does not mean great wisdom. What lay ahead in Japan?

On May 6, 1709, we landed at Nagasaki in Japan. I had been to many strange places, but Japan may have been the strangest. It also may have been their language. I had learned many languages. They all had

---

1. immortality having the quality of not dying

certain things in common. However, Japanese was like no other language I have studied.

It took me two weeks of travel to reach the capital. I presented my letter. I spoke to the emperor in Low Dutch, which he understood and spoke well. I told him the story I had made up.

I was supposed to be a shipwrecked Dutch sailor. I had been stranded in Luggnagg. There, I learned that Luggnagg and Japan had a trading agreement, and I knew Japan traded with the Dutch. I asked the emperor for permission to take the next boat for Holland.

Now came the tricky part. I had been warned about this by the king of Luggnagg. A regular part of meeting him was to trample a cross underfoot. If this was not done, there would be no trading with the Japanese.

Being a good Christian, this was unthinkable to me. I explained that I was not in Japan to trade goods. I was there by accident. Would I still have to trample a cross?

I was happily surprised. The emperor was friendly. He did not even have me trample a cross to show I was not a Christian. My papers allowed me to board a Dutch ship, bound for Amsterdam. From there, I easily got a boat to England. I arrived there with no money. But I felt that what I had learned was worth much more.

PART FOUR:
A VOYAGE TO HOUYHNHNM LAND

1 Among the Gentle Horse People

When I returned to England, I was greeted warmly by my wife. I had a good life for five months. But after all the strange lands I had seen, England was boring. As ever, money became a problem. In my travels, I had learned much but earned little. Then a lucky chance came my way.

I was asked to go to sea again. I had had my fill of being a ship's doctor. I was offered the chance to be a captain. I could not resist. When a merchant ship has a successful voyage, the captain gets most of the money. I must also admit that the idea of being in command was appealing to me.

So it was that I set sail in 1710, as captain of the ship *Adventure*. She was a good sound ship, with a fine crew. All went well until we left Teneriffe, off the Canary Islands.[1] A great storm came up. I lost several men. I was forced to put in at the Barbados Islands[2] to get new crewmen.

I did not care for the look of these new men. However, I had little choice. A successful voyage was first in my mind. We still had to reach the Bay of Campechy, off Mexico. There we were to pick up our cargo of logs. We would then return to England, and I would be rich.

It did not turn out that way. We had been at sea

---

1. **Canary Islands** islands in the Atlantic, off the northwest coast of Africa
2. **Barbados Islands** islands in the British West Indies

only a short time when I discovered the truth. The new men were not honest sailors at all. They were a band of pirates! In the dark of night, they took over the ship, killing many men. I fought as best I could, but sunrise found me their prisoner.

Perhaps because I had treated all my men well, the pirates did not kill me, too. What they did was almost as bad. They put me ashore on the rocky coast of the first island they found. I had only my clothes and my sword. They kept my pistol. My heart sank as I saw the *Adventure* sail off. I knew not where I was. What would become of me?

I decided to explore this island. Perhaps there were people. There might even be a harbor where I could get a ship for home. I was soon disappointed. By good luck, there were plenty of fruit trees. I did not have to worry about food. There were also many streams so that water was no problem, either. But were there people? Were there animals?

In the forest, I came across many animal tracks. I could not figure out what sort of animals had made them. In fact, I did not know if the animals were still alive. The tracks may have been very old. Some of the tracks looked like those of horses that wore no shoes, but wild horses were not native to these islands. Other tracks were a total mystery to me. They were too strange to figure out.

I was walking into a small clearing when I saw a group of strange animals. Some were seated on the ground. A few were in trees. I must confess that they were the ugliest things I have ever seen. They looked like hairy monkeys with no tails. There was a terrible smell in the air. It must have come from these animals.

One of them spotted me and ran at me. I was so

disgusted that I struck at it with my sword. Suddenly, they all began to attack me. I cut left and right with my blade. They were trying to form a circle around me. If they did that, I would be lost. I got my back against a tree trunk. From there, I defended myself.

I was still not safe. There were animals in the tree above me. They began to throw filth down upon my head. I do not know how long I fought. Finally, they gave up and ran off into the forest. I was nearly spent and sank to the ground. I heard a strange sound— heavy footsteps. I looked up and was amazed at what I saw. I was face to face with a very large horse!

The animal had large intelligent eyes. It was looking at me in wonder. It gave a whinny and looked over its shoulder. Another horse joined it. The two of them looked at me as if I had fallen to earth from the moon. To my amazement, they seemed to be talking to each other about me.

When I listened closely, I could make out words. These were horses like none I had even known. I could make out two words in their language: *Yahoo* and *Houyhnhnm*. But what these meant, I could not tell.

They examined my clothing, which seemed to puzzle them. I spoke to them in whatever languages I knew. It did not help. But they did seem surprised that I spoke at all. They again fell to talking to each other. With gentle signs and looks, they showed that they wanted me to follow them. I did so.

We walked a fair distance to a village. I had never seen such a place. All the people were horses. The buildings were made of wood, very clean and straight. Their houses had no steps. Instead, they had ramps—easy for horses to climb. I knew not the name of the first horse I had met. He gave me to understand that I was to go with him. The other went about his business.

For all their size, these creatures were gentle. The entire town was peaceful and calm. In any English village, there would have been noises and cries. Here there was only a gentle whinny and sweet nods of greeting to my guide. I followed him into a neat house.

The inside was neat and clean as the streets of the village. It was apparent that my guide had a family. I saw a lovely gray mare and a dark-haired colt. They were seated on straw mats. About them was furniture of wood and straw. All was clean and orderly. As I came into the room, the mare rose to her feet. She, like the other horses, looked at me in wonder.

She went straight to her colt, as though to protect it. A quick series of whinnies must have put her mind at rest. However, she stayed close to the colt. From time to time, she would nuzzle it and make comforting sounds to it. I was puzzled. Why should these lovely, gentle creatures fear me? I was small and weak.

My guide made a sign that I was to follow him. He led me outside to a hut. I looked in horror. Inside the hut were more of the horrid, ugly creatures that had attacked me. They had been disgusting in the open countryside. Kept indoors, their habits were worse. They were covered in filth and fought among themselves. The cries and smell were enough to make one sick.

I was ready to run. If my guide wanted to put me in that hut, I would rather die. I was fighting hard not to be sick. But to my relief, we went right by the hut. My horse guide led me to a building between the house and the smelly hut. The inside was crude, but quite clean.

My guide left me there. A short time later, a servant horse came. It dropped my dinner before me. My stomach twisted. It was rotten meat. Then I recognized the smell. It was the same as from the hut. The horses were feeding me what they gave to those awful beasts. There was no way I could eat that, either.

The horses dined on hay. I could not eat this. I made signs to the servant that I could not eat the rotten meat. He took it away. In a while, he came back with a dish of oats and milk. It was hardly a human meal. But I had eaten cooked oats before. I knew from my medical training that I could live on this diet. I ate what I could. So ended my first day in this strange land.

The next day, my diet was better. My guide soon discovered that I knew how to use fire. This was something that the ugly creatures knew not. I was able to toast my oats and heat my milk. I soon had a hearty breakfast of oatmeal.

It was that very day that my guide set out to teach me the horse language. As I have explained, I have a gift for languages. We soon were able to speak in simple terms. The horse language was like High Dutch in some ways.

I soon learned a great deal. The horse creatures were called Houyhnhnms. They ruled this land. The ugly, filthy animals were called Yahoos. The Houyhnhnms used the Yahoos as beasts of burden. I discovered this during one of my lessons.

An important guest came to call. He arrived in a kind of big sled, with a ramp at its end. The sled was being pulled by a team of four Yahoos. It was apparent that this was a very important Houyhnhnm. He had many servants who walked behind the sled. With great respect, he was shown into the building that housed me.

Again, I saw the look of wonder on a Houyhnhnm face. I was able to pick out a few words as the very important Houyhnhnm spoke to my guide. They were talking about my clothes. No Yahoo ever wore clothes. What they couldn't get over was my gloves. I took them off and put them on again. That was good for a few minutes of conversation among the Houyhnhnms.

I soon understood what they were talking about. They were trying to decide if I was a new sort of creature or just a different sort of Yahoo. I had heard words like this in Brobdingnag. There, they decided I was an odd sort of splacknuck. To the giants, I was always an animal, though a strange one. What would be the decision of the Houyhnhnms? I decided to see if I could make them understand. When the very important Houyhnhnm left, I was alone with my guide. If I could show him I was intelligent, I could prove I was not a Yahoo.

I began to tell him about where I came from. I told him of the strange places I had visited. I mentioned that I was going to put all my experiences into a book. He stopped me. He asked me what a book was! It seemed that the Houyhnhnms have no written language. I put together some things to write with. My guide was impressed, up to a point. He asked what the purpose of books was.

I told him books were a way to record the truth. They would tell others about events that took place. That way, no one could get away with lies. My mind flashed back to Glubbdubdrib. It was there that I had learned that history can be lies. I did not mention this to my guide. I had to prove I was no Yahoo.

2 Imitating the Houyhnhnms

I had to marvel at the Houyhnhnm society. They had no idea what a lie was. My guide was really puzzled about lies. He told me that the purpose of language is to communicate. Lying is the opposite of communicating. Any idea of a lie was unthinkable.

What a race these horses were! They had no books, yet they were wise. The Houyhnhnms knew nothing of war and crime. Without lies, there was little use for politics.

Finally, my guide told me something I will never forget. He saw no use for writing or history. These things were of no use to these wonderful horse people. They were ruled by reason alone. All important matters were decided by it. All the "glorious" things I had spoken of had little meaning to the Houyhnhnms.

My second day of education had ended. I felt I had given little of value to my guide. I had gotten much of value from him.

My education continued. The next day, I set out to explain English history. I spoke of England's many victories in wars. Again, I was stopped. I had to explain what a war was. My guide listened. I could tell by the look on his face that he was puzzled. The look turned to horror. I felt it best to change the subject.

I then spoke to him of the rich and the poor. He asked me to explain. I told him simply: If you are rich, you have money. But the Houyhnhnms use no money. They have no idea what it is.

I tried simpler terms: The rich can eat, and the poor cannot. This, too, was beyond him. He replied that if any Houyhnhnm is hungry, he eats. If he has no food handy, the other Houyhnhnms feed him. In this marvelous land, there was no such thing as money or hunger.

I was still intent on showing my guide that humans were not Yahoos. But with each question he asked, it was getting harder to prove. Man is not a perfect creature. But these horse people seemed close to perfection. I later learned that their very name—*Houyhnhnm*—means "perfection in Nature." I find it hard to disprove.

I then tried another approach. I told my guide that I was a doctor. Surely, this would impress him. He asked me what doctors did. I explained that doctors can tell what sickness a person has. A doctor can tell if a person will live or die. Doctors have great knowledge, I told him.

He wanted to know what doctors *do*, besides saying when someone will die. Could they do anything about it? I felt my face grow warm. I had to admit that we doctors can very rarely help the sick. Then what was the use of doctors, my guide asked. I couldn't give him a good answer.

I tried to talk to him about politics in England. It was of no use. The lies, the stealing, the betrayals were all strange to him. In the end, I felt I had made no headway. I felt more and more like a Yahoo myself.

The days passed into months. My education continued. With each day, I felt more impressed by these Houyhnhnms. I began to give up the idea of proving I was special. In the end, I knew what I wanted to do.

I asked my guide's permission to stay among

the Houyhnhnms. I would do my best to be like them in every way. After learning about these wonderful horse people, I felt that England seemed a terrible place. Why return to sickness? Why go back to crime, lies, and wars? What need did I have for money in Houyhnhnm Land? The place was a heaven on earth.

My guide listened and at first said nothing. Then he spoke to me at length. He said it was difficult to believe all he had heard from me. I had started out saying how wonderful man was. I had said that doctors were great men. I had praised England and its history. Then, after my guide had asked me a few simple questions, I had to take back all I had said.

The way that my guide saw it was clear. He thought it was possible that I was not a Yahoo. He also felt that men and Yahoos were very much alike. It was as though there was something negative in man's blood. It made him more like a Yahoo than a Houyhnhnm.

I had to defend myself. I spoke of the Yahoos. They were greedy, I said. They collected shiny stones and hid them away. They would steal the stones from each other. They would even kill to get them.

I went on. The Yahoos chose the worst and nastiest of their kind for leaders. They are dirty. They have diseases. I finished by saying that a pig is a sweet, clean creature beside a Yahoo. The guide said nothing.

Then I thought of man. Diamonds are shiny stones. Men will steal and kill for them. Many of man's leaders have been nasty and cruel. London has many diseases. I thought of all that went on in England. I had no real answer. Perhaps my Houyhnhnm guide was right.

I began to think. Perhaps the Yahoos acted as they

did because they were treated as animals. What they were like in their own society was not known to me. I asked permission of my guide to visit the Yahoos. He had some fears about this but agreed. He sent with me his servant, the Sorrel Nag, to protect me.

We came upon the place where the Yahoos lived. I did not know what to expect. The last time I had seen them, I had had to fight them off. To my surprise, I was welcomed.

They were very curious about me. Mostly, it was my clothing that drew their attention. As I have said, the Yahoos wear none. They are covered in hairy fur, except for their rears. They crowded about me, but did not seem dangerous.

I had a chance to see how these creatures lived. It is still upsetting for me to think about. They had no village, unlike the Houyhnhnms. They lived in holes in the ground. They changed to new holes often. The smell made me understand why. Yahoos are not housebroken. What is worse is that they fight among themselves constantly. When they do, they throw their own filth at each other.

I had a chance to see what they ate. They lived on frogs, fish, and whatever dead animals they come across. They seem to have no real government. The biggest and cruelest Yahoo becomes their leader.

They have no family life. They make no connection between their actions and having children. A female Yahoo would find herself with child, but would not know how or why. Sometimes they would care for their offspring. Sometimes they did not. I saw bands of Yahoo children with no parents.

The young Yahoos acted no differently than the adults. I could not tell if they acted as they did because they saw how the adults acted. Perhaps my

Houyhnhnm guide was right when he said that it is in the Yahoo blood to be filthy, greedy, and cruel.

To my horror, the Yahoos acted like I was one of them. I could go nowhere without a group of them following me. The closeness of them made me feel dirty.

Once, I went to a nearby stream and went for a swim. I could not have done a worse thing. As soon as they saw me naked, there was no stopping them. One really ugly female began to go after me.

It was the Sorrel Nag who saved me. I then returned to the stream bank and put on my clothes. The Yahoos were still all around me. Now they were sure I was also a Yahoo. They had seen me without clothing. They felt I was one of them, but was putting on airs. This seemed to make them really angry. They began to scream at me. They threw their filth at me.

With the Sorrel Nag to protect me, I made my way back to the Houyhnhnm village. The peace of the village was like heaven to me. But I noticed there was hardly a horse person to be seen. I asked the Sorrel Nag about this. He told me that the Houyhnhnms were at a meeting.

I thought of how different it was here compared to where the Yahoos live. The Houyhnhnms eat only the cleanest of food. They have real houses. Though they have servants, like the Sorrel Nag, all Houyhnhnms are equals.

No Houyhnhnm marries for money; they have none. They do not marry for love, either. They do not feel that love is a reasonable state of mind. They marry in the same way that men breed horses. The strongest and best looking marry each other. But in the case of the Houyhnhnms, they also value intelligence.

The Houyhnhnm children are raised with great care. This is not done because they are loved. It is done because the young will one day rule their land. The adults take great care to see that the children learn well. They feel that an educated society is a society ruled by reason.

The Houyhnhnms have no government, as such. With no lies, no money, and no poverty, there is little to talk about. As they have no wars or crime, there are no laws against such things. Why pass laws against something that does not exist?

What the Houyhnhnms do is to follow pure reason. What seems reasonable to be done is what is done, and there are no arguments about this. For this reason, they meet only once every four years. The meetings are always short. But there was a meeting going on this day. What could be the reason?

When my guide returned, I discovered the cause of the meeting. The Houyhnhnms were concerned about the Yahoos. I learned something that the Sorrel Nag had not told me.

The Yahoos were not native to Houyhnhnm Land. It seems that they just appeared one day in the mountains. Since that time, they had multiplied and grown greatly in numbers. Packs of Yahoos could be dangerous. I had learned that earlier.

The only reason that the Houyhnhnms kept the Yahoos around was a logical one. Even though Yahoos could not be housebroken, they could be trained as beasts of burden. I had seen this. When the very important Houyhnhnm visited my guide, his sled was pulled by Yahoos.

The Houyhnhnms said that they had made a mistake with the Yahoos. Donkeys are native to

Houyhnhnm Land. They should have trained donkeys instead. But what were they to do about all these Yahoos?

My guide had spoken at the meeting. He explained what I had told him about England. I had almost forgotten it. I had told him about horses in England and how men raised and bred them. I listened in horror to what my master said.

He told the meeting that in England, Yahoos **neuter**[1] horses. He said that it seemed logical that the Houyhnhnms should neuter Yahoos here. If the Yahoos could not breed, they would die off after a number of years. I had seen young colts neutered. That was one thing. But the idea of doing this to an adult— even a Yahoo—was scary.

One could well ask why the idea filled me with dread. After all, my guide had said all this in his usual logical way. The reason that I was worried was a simple one. To the Houyhnhnms, I was a Yahoo. Would I be neutered, too?

I tried to find this out. My guide would say no more about what went on at the meeting. I did not know if the plan to neuter the Yahoos had been approved. If so, when would the plan be set into action?

I made a plan of my own. In the months that followed, I tried my best to become a Houyhnhnm. I imitated the Houyhnhnm walk. I tried to make my speech and voice more like theirs. I tried to learn all that I could about their society. There, problems arose. As I have explained, the Houyhnhnms have no written language. I could not study their history. Anything I learned had to come from my guide or from a servant horse. I did my best to spend as much time with my guide as I could.

---

1. **neuter** making neither male nor female

3 *I Become a Threat*

The way that I imitated Houyhnhnms seemed to work. I was given a small room of my own inside the guide's house. Using some crude tools, I ground my oats into flour. I soon was eating real bread. I also discovered some honey bees, so I had something to eat on my bread.

Because I was clean and did not break into their conversation, I was allowed at Houyhnhnm dinners. When this happened, I studied all that was said very carefully. I was set on becoming a Houyhnhnm myself.

One night at dinner, I learned that a Houyhnhnms had died. I wondered what the horse people did when this happened.

It was most interesting. The dead Houyhnhnm were buried. That was it. There were no words spoken and no praying. There also was no crying and carrying on. They accepted death as the end of life. It was natural, and it was logical. I thought of funerals I had been to in England. An English funeral was something a Yahoo would do.

I learned more. The Houyhnhnms don't have calendars. They do not count years, only months. They care little of objects in the sky. But they do know what an eclipse is and why it happens. They had enough science for their simple needs.

To my delight, my efforts to be Houyhnhnm-like pleased my guide. Each day, in every way, I tried to be more horse-like. I fancied my whinny was getting better, too. I suppose I was getting to be a bit of a showoff. It ended up causing problems.

One evening, the very important Houyhnhnm came to dinner. He arrived as usual, in his sled drawn by Yahoos. I did not go outside the house to greet him. It would have meant seeing and smelling the Yahoos. My thinking was getting more Houyhnhnm-like. My horror of the Yahoos grew. In the Houyhnhnm language, the only word for *evil* is *Yahoo.*

At dinner, I did not remain silent. I took part in the talk. I showed off my best eating manners. I spoke of how I admired Houyhnhnm society. I told the very important Houyhnhnm how much I hated Yahoos— even those in England.

The very important Houyhnhnm asked me more about England. I talked in my best Houyhnhnm accent of my own country. I spoke of how there was crime, poverty, and lies. I explained about money and what lack of it can do. I talked of how men got money. But this time I was careful not to speak of how men bred horses.

When I finished, I was quite pleased with myself. I had seen the very important Houyhnhnm nod his head once in a while during my speech. At the end of the meal, I was sent to my room. My guide and the very important Houyhnhnm had things to talk over in private.

The next day, the Sorrel Nag came to my room. The guide wished to speak to me. I was quite happy. I felt it had to do with my speech the night before. Maybe I had shown the very important Houyhnhnm how horse-like I had become? The thoughts of being neutered seemed far away. I could not have been more wrong!

My guide began to talk. Yes, I had impressed the very important Houyhnhnm. I had done more than that. I had frightened him. In spite of all my learning and trying to be a Houyhnhnm, he still thought I was a Yahoo. A dangerous one!

I asked why he thought that I was dangerous. My guide replied that it was my intelligence. The Houyhnhnms thought of the Yahoos as stupid, filthy, ugly beasts. I agreed with this. Surely I had shown I was none of these things.

My guide went on. Because I was so smart and clean, I could be a threat. I knew Houyhnhnm language. I knew Houyhnhnm society. I could become a leader of all the Yahoos. I could start a revolution. The Houyhnhnms are a gentle folk. They know not of war or violence. What could they do to stop me?

I thought for a time. It was as though a man had discovered a very clever rat. The rat could speak. The rat could learn. The rat could teach other rats. It could lead others. Also, rats breed fast. One clever rat could have all London under its control in a few years. As ever, the Houyhnhnm logic was sound.

But what would become of me, I asked. My guide had been given two choices by the Houyhnhnms. This had already happened at their meeting. The important Houyhnhnm had come to dinner to make sure of what had been decided. My showing off had confirmed what the meeting had decided.

I was given two choices. I could no longer be a pet Yahoo. I would have to live with the other Yahoos. I would have no further contact with Houyhnhnms. They did not say it, but I had another thought: The Houyhnhnms intended to neuter all Yahoos soon. I would be among that number.

My second choice was to swim back to England! As smart as the Houyhnhnms were, they had no idea of boats or ships. They had no need for such things. They did know what swimming was. They reasoned that if I had come from the sea, as I had said, I must have swum here. So naturally, I could swim back.

I tried to explain to my guide that this was impossible. I needed a boat of some sort. But to explain a boat to a Houyhnhnm was like explaining money or violence. I finally got through. I told him I needed to build a *thing* that would make me swim better.

During the time before the meeting, I was allowed to roam Houyhnhnm Land freely. Once, I had gone to the seashore. At that time, I had seen another island, far away. I had not thought of it for some time. I was so happy trying to be a Houyhnhnm. Who would ever want to leave? But now it was important for me to do so.

The Houyhnhnms had only the simplest of tools. That was all they needed for their simple buildings. Somehow, I managed to use them. I built the frame of a small boat. I covered this with animal skins. I plugged the holes with mud and fat.

I did not know how far this boat would carry me. I was not sure that it would work at all. I had no choice. The idea of living the rest of my life as a Yahoo disgusted me. The time had come to leave.

My heart was heavy as I said my good-byes. I walked once more through the streets of the village. I admired the graceful walk of the horse people. I still imitated them as I walked.

When I reached my guide's house, I was greeted by the faithful Sorrel Nag. He showed me into my guide's room.

I told my guide how I wished I could stay. He replied that it was impossible. I asked then for one favor. He said if it was reasonable, he would grant me the favor. I told him I wanted only to kneel before him and to kiss his hoof. This seemed reasonable, and he allowed it.

The Sorrel Nag walked with me to the shore. I hoped it was because he had come to like me. Or it may have been my guide's wish. I was to be protected from the Yahoos. The Sorrel Nag seemed interested in my boat, but not very.

We said our good-byes. I pushed my boat into the water. It floated! I raised my sail of animal skin, and the boat began to move. The Sorrel Nag stood on the shore watching in wonder. He was still there when Houyhnhnm Land faded from my view.

4 Returning to England

I soon found that my sail was of little use. The wind tore it apart. I had to paddle. After a day's paddling, I reached the island that I had seen. I pulled my boat ashore and began to explore this new place. I knew not what I would find.

The island had trees, which was good. That meant there would be water. I still had oats and bread in my boat. They would not last forever. I found a clear stream. I took a chance and tried the water. It was good tasting, and I had no problems.

I began to search for food. I hoped for fruit trees of some kind. After my time with the horse people, the idea of eating meat turned my stomach. I found seashells all over the shore, but no shellfish to eat.

Beyond the shore lay a forest. There could be anything living in it. I still had my sword. But what good would it do against a truly large beast? There could even be herds of beasts. Even worse, this might be where the Yahoos had come from years ago. I was tired from my voyage. I turned my boat over me for shelter and went to sleep.

The next morning, I ate my oats and checked my sword. I could put it off no longer. I went into the forest. I wandered about for hours. I marked trees so I could find my way back to my boat.

I entered a small clearing. From there, about 500 yards away, I saw smoke. I moved closer. On a small hill were a group of island natives. To my relief, they were not Yahoos. But they wore no clothing at all.

There were about 20 of them: men, women, and children. I moved as close as I could to see more of them. I came too close. One of the men spotted me. He spoke rapidly to the others. My heart sank when I saw the men pick up bows and arrows. I ran.

The natives followed. I was not used to running through a forest. I had gotten used to the straight, flat farmland of the Houyhnhnms. I fell several times. Once, I ran into a tree. Each time that I lost ground, the natives got closer.

I broke out of the forest and onto the shore. I turned my boat right-side up and pushed off into the sea. The natives were hot behind me. I was now beyond the reach of their hands. Was I safe?

Suddenly, I felt a pain behind my left knee. I looked down and saw a native arrow, deep in my leg. I paddled as hard as I could. Arrows fell around me like rain. At last I was beyond their range.

The natives stood on the shore for a time, crying out in anger. I stayed away from the shore for hours. I cut the arrow from my leg, using my sword. With great pain, I took care of my wound and dressed it. Still the natives stood there in anger.

I raised my ragged sail. There was a light breeze. It did not tear the sail. I moved off and lost sight of the island. I was in great pain. To make it worse, I had had no time to bring water with me, though I still had oats, bread, and honey.

I spent the night going where the wind took me. In the morning, I spotted a sail! It was clearly a ship from Europe. I was about to try to make a signal, but I then stopped myself. I began to think.

This was a European ship. It might even be English. It could carry me home. But where was home, really? I thought of London. There would be crime, violence, and poverty. There would be dirt, rats, and filth. There would be politics and lies.

I thought of the wonderful land of the Houyhnhnms. After my time there, going back to England would be terrible. How different were the English or all Europeans from Yahoos? I made up my mind. I gave no signal to the ship. I headed back toward the island. I would rather live among natives than among European Yahoos.

I landed under cover of darkness. There was no sign of the natives. There was no fire I could see. My knee hurt terribly. I felt a heat in my body like a fever. My wound may have been infected, and I knew not if the arrow had been poisoned. I passed out on the sandy shore.

When I awoke, there were still no natives in sight. Then I saw the ship from the day before. It was close to shore. They were putting a boat into the water. In spite of the pain in my leg, I ran into the forest to hide. I would not go back to Europe if I could help it.

I followed the stream into the forest and found a place to hide behind a rock. This did me no good. The very reason that the men had come ashore was to get fresh water. This place was well known to sailors, it seemed.

I later found out that they were looking for me, anyway. They had found my boat. They knew the natives of this island had no knowledge of boat making. From the way my boat was made, they knew it was European. They found my hiding place.

I stood up as best I could. One of the sailors spoke to me. I knew his language right way. It was Portuguese. I know this tongue well. I told him in his own language to leave me alone. I was just a poor

Yahoo, far from Houyhnhnm Land. I could not go back there. I wished to live alone.

Their mouths dropped open in surprise. They saw my odd clothes. They were amazed at how strange I looked. What got to them most was the way I talked. I had spent five years among the Houyhnhnms. I now had an accent.

They knew I was speaking Portuguese. But my whinnying and neighing way of talking puzzled them. It was as though in England a dog began to bark in English. In my case, it was like a horse was talking Portuguese. They had no idea what a Yahoo or a Houyhnhnm was. They may have thought I was crazy.

The sailor in charge spoke to me. He told me that my wound would need attention. His ship's captain would also want to see me. He also wanted to know what strange country I was from. He had never heard anyone talk Portuguese like a horse would!

I was brought aboard the Portuguese ship. I spoke with the captain. I managed to convince him I was English. I told him only a little of my five-year stay in Houyhnhnm Land. I recalled how I was not believed in the past about strange lands I had visited.

The captain was most kind. He said that Portugal and England were not enemies at this time. He would bring me to Lisbon, the capital of Portugal, for free. From there, he told me, I could find an English ship. I could then get back to London. I finally gave in.

All this took place some years ago. I reached London safely. My wife and family were overjoyed to see me alive. I was less than happy. I could not bear the sights, sounds, and smells of London. Much as I loved my wife, she reminded me that I was a Yahoo.

I could not live in my own house. I moved into the stables. True, these horses could not speak. But their

appearance and gentle ways made me feel better. I ate simple food as I had in Houyhnhnm Land: oats, bread, and honey. From time to time, I wept. I was a Yahoo in a land of Yahoos.

With love and great patience, my wife brought me back to being a man. After a year, I moved back into my house. I again took up my profession as a doctor. This time, I was successful because I also treated horses. Everyone marveled at how well I understood the creatures.

So I have returned to being a man. I hope I am a much wiser man for my travels. I have tried to teach my children the gentle ways and sweet reason of the Houyhnhnms. I have taught them to prize truth. I hope I have succeeded.

I know that many will not believe what I have written on these pages. I maintain that every word is the truth. Though I may be but an English Yahoo, I have lived among the Houyhnhnms. I cannot lie. I would have no reason to lie.

It is my hope that anyone who reads this will be the wiser for the reading. I also hope that anyone who writes of his travels will be just as honest. I have learned that books often contain lies. This is for a number of reasons. Some writers tell people only what they wish to hear. Others will not tell the truth because they fear they will not be believed. Still others lie for profit and because, at heart, they are Yahoos. I will have none of them and wish never to see them.

REVIEWING YOUR READING
PART ONE: A VOYAGE TO LILLIPUT
CHAPTERS 1–2

FINDING THE MAIN IDEA

1. The Lilliputians were tiny
a) and had nothing in common with Gulliver b) but were as strong as Gulliver c) but injured Gulliver badly d) but behaved like ordinary humans in many ways.

REMEMBERING DETAILS

2. The Lilliputians captured Gulliver by
a) using their army b) tricking him c) tying him down while he slept d) shooting him with arrows.

3. After Gulliver is given drugged wine, he is
a) tied down more firmly. b) hoisted onto a cart and carried away c) robbed d) released.

4. Gulliver is first housed by the Lilliptians in
a) a condemned building b) the palace c) an empty house d) a ship.

5. Gulliver shows he is not dangerous by
a) pretending to eat some little archers b) smiling c) showing he has no weapons d) dancing.

6. When Gulliver steals the Blefuscudian navy, he protects his eyes from arrows by
a) using his hands b) swimming underwater c) closing his eyes d) wearing eyeglasses.

7. Gulliver is almost put to death because
a) he doesn't show enough respect b) he tries to escape c) he won't destroy the cities of Belfuscu d) politicians accuse him of treason.

DRAWING CONCLUSIONS

8. Gulliver concludes that the emperor feels self-important because
a) he has a very long name and title b) he makes a grand entrance c) he makes a long speech d) all of the above.

9. Gulliver is given a certain amount of food and drink
a) according to his size b) for performing services for the country c) because the Lilliputians don't want him to starve d) so he will stay in Lilliput.

USING YOUR REASONING

10. The Lilliputians hide all of Gulliver's personal effects because
    a) they are valuable b) he has weapons c) they aren't sure what they are d) they enjoy tricking him.

11. The Lilliputians, as part of Gulliver's parole, make him stay on roads so he
    a) won't trample farmland or animals b) is easier to see c) can move faster that way d) can see more of Lilliput.

THINKING IT OVER

12. Two Lilliputian practices stand out to Gulliver as being extremely foolish. One has to do with how political appointments are made. The other has to do with a religious argument. Describe each one and explain what they reveal about the Lilliputians, who display such dignity and self-important airs.

CHAPTERS 3–4

FINDING THE MAIN IDEA

1. Why do Flimnap and Bolgolam become Gulliver's enemies?
   a) Gulliver has become a national hero. b) Gulliver has done their jobs better than they. c) They are afraid that the emperor likes Gulliver better than them. d) all of the above.

REMEMBERING DETAILS

2. When Gulliver steals the navy of Blefuscu, he protects his eyes from arrows with
   a) his hands b) a helmet c) his eyeglasses.

3. For his deeds, the emperor
   a) makes Gulliver a knight b) gives him the title of *Nardac*
   c) gives him money d) gives him a party.

4. Flimnap and Bolgolam do not accuse Gulliver of
   a) being too easy on the Blefuscudians b) stealing from the treasury c) costing too much to feed d) treason.

5. Gulliver escapes by
   a) repairing his own lifeboat b) building a raft c) swimming
   d) riding a dolphin.

DRAWING CONCLUSIONS

6. Gulliver says that all Lilliputian laws are not silly. Many are good and sound. He feels this way because
   a) Reldresal explains them better b) laws change with the times
   c) he compares them with English laws and finds many are harsher d) none of the above.

USING YOUR REASONING

7. Gulliver gains respect for Reldresal because he
   a) holds a high government job b) wears the finest clothes
   c) dares to tell Gulliver the truth about the emperor d) can speak English.

8. Lilliputians care little for their children. They show this by
   a) beating them b) sending them to boarding school for years
   c) refusing to feed them d) ignoring them.

THINKING IT OVER

9. Though Gulliver commits a number of acts of violence, he is really a man of peace. Find evidence in the text that this is true.

PART TWO: A VOYAGE TO BROBDINGNAG
CHAPTERS 1–4

FINDING THE MAIN IDEA

1. Gulliver is never regarded as a human by the giant farmer because
   a) there is a man-like animal in Brobdingnag b) he is too small to be taken seriously c) he doesn't behave like one of them
   d) he wears strange clothes.

REMEMBERING DETAILS

2. Gulliver goes to sea again aboard a ship named
   a) the *Antelope* b) the *Pilgrim* c) the *Adventure* d) the *Voyager*.

3. He is captured by a farmhand in
   a) the ocean, off the island b) in a field of giant wheat c) a huge mousetrap d) a barn.

4. Gulliver is first made a pet by
   a) the queen of Brobdingnag b) the farmer's daughter
   c) the farmer's wife d) the farmer.

5. Gulliver fights off an attack by
   a) the farmer's cat b) giant rats c) giant cockroaches d) a giant dog.

6. Gulliver falls ill after
   a) perfoming in many shows b) performing for the queen
   c) catching a cold d) being bitten by a giant flea.

DRAWING CONCLUSIONS

7. When Gulliver is attacked by the queen's dwarf, he does not tell what happened because
a) he doesn't want to snitch b) he understands why the dwarf did it c) they are both little people in a giant land d) he is so scared, he can't tell.

USING YOUR REASONING

8. When Gulliver is given a boat to sail on the pond, it is very badly made. This is because
a) it is only a toy b) the giants can't make a good one so small c) Brobdingnag has no navy d) no one knew how to build one properly.

9. Gulliver cannot stand the sight of the beggars when he tours the land with the king. This is because
a) they are so ugly and deformed b) their cries for money hurt his ears c) they have giant fleas d) all of the above.

10. Gulliver thinks he can make a fortune back in England by
a) telling his story b) working as a doctor c) selling the luxurious possessions the Brobdingnagian craftsmen had made d) all of the above.

THINKING IT OVER

11. Gulliver decides that though they are huge, the giant people are not as cruel as the Lilliputians. Find evidence in the text to support this.

PART THREE: A VOYAGE TO LAPUTA
CHAPTERS 1–2

FINDING THE MAIN IDEA

1. Gulliver discovers that whole countries can be so specialized that they are ineffective. He knows this from
a) his voyage to Laputa, where everyone is a thinker, and Balnibarbi, where everyone is good at details b) his trip to the immortal Struldbruggs c) his visit with the Luggnaggians, who hated the English d) his visit with the magicians of Glubbdugdrib.

REMEMBERING DETAILS

2. The great thinkers of Laputa are always accompanied by
a) servants called Flappers b) their pet dogs c) their spouses d) their friends.

3. The island of Laputa floats by
   a) use of a huge magnet b) helium balloons c) magic d) air
   currents.
4. Gulliver gets onto Laputa with the help of
   a) a balloon b) a chair on pulleys c) birds d) an elevator.
5. The Laputans wear clothing covered with
   a) patches b) embroidery c) symbols d) buttons.
6. The buildings of Balnibarbi are falling down because
   a) the people are poor workmen b) the materials are shoddy
   c) the plans for them are bad d) the people are not smart.
7. When people approach the king of Luggnagg, they have to
   a) bow b) give him money c) praise him d) lick the floor.
8. The Struldbruggs live forever, but Gulliver finds they are
   a) very wise b) very strong c) very old but neither strong nor
   wise d) none of the above.

DRAWING CONCLUSIONS

9. The Laputans, though they are great thinkers, are not
   efficient because
   a) they don't put their knowledge to practical use b) they never
   start a project c) they use the people of Balnibarbi for servants
   d) they are lazy.
10. Gulliver concludes that living forever is not so desirable
    because he
    a) sees what the Struldbruggs have become b) would get bored
    c) would run out of money d) would become ill forever.
11. Gulliver concludes that the emperor of Japan is a reasonable
    man because
    a) he hates Christians b) he believes Gulliver's story
    c) Gulliver does not have to trample a cross underfoot
    d) he asks Gulliver all about his travels.

USING YOUR REASONING

12. The people of Balnibarbi are not poor workmen. They follow
    the Laputans' plans because
    a) the Laputans are smart b) they can't draw up their own plans
    c) if they don't, the Laputans will bomb them with stones
    d) all of the above.

13. The ghosts of Glubbdubdrig show Gulliver that
    a) life was best in ancient times b) Caesar was greater than Brutus
    c) Aristotle was a wise man d) history is often a pack of lies.

THINKING IT OVER

14. After visiting these strange lands with people who have great powers, Gulliver becomes convinced that being an ordinary human without special powers isn't so bad after all. Find evidence in the text to support this.

PART FOUR: A VOYAGE TO HOUYHNHNM LAND
CHAPTERS 1–4

FINDING THE MAIN IDEA

1. Gulliver discovers that perhaps people are not more advanced than animals when
   a) he returns to England b) he is attacked by Yahoos c) he sees how wise and gentle the Houyhnhnms are d) none of the above.

REMEMBERING DETAILS

2. Gulliver is aboard the *Adventure* as
   a) ship's doctor b) captain c) first officer d) a passenger.
3. Some of his men turn out to be
   a) pirates b) sick with fever c) French d) unskilled.
4. According to the map, in what body of water is Houyhnhnm Land located?
   a) the Atlantic Ocean b) the Caribbean Sea c) the Pacific Ocean d) the Mediterranean Sea.
5. When Gulliver first lands on the island, he is attacked by
   a) birds b) Houyhnhnms c) Yahoos d) pirates.
6. The horse people use Yahoos for
   a) carrying things b) food c) pets d) sports.
7. From what country was the ship that picked up Gulliver?
   a) France b) England c) Portugal d) Spain.
8. Gulliver is attacked by island natives and wounded in
   a) the chest b) the leg c) the arm d) the back.
9. Gulliver's homemade canoe is covered with
   a) birch bark b) wood c) animal skins d) cloth.

10. When Gulliver returns to England, he first lives
    a) in his house b) in an apartment in London c) in the stables
    d) in a tent.

DRAWING CONCLUSIONS

11. Gulliver concludes that the Houyhnhnms are better than men because they
    a) are bigger and stronger b) are ruled by pure logic c) eat no meat d) live longer.

12. Gulliver concludes that he must prove to the Houyhnhnms that he is not a Yahoo because
    a) he looks so much like one b) the Yahoos are so disgusting
    c) the Yahoos act like men in so many ways d) he wants to become a Houyhnhnm.

USING YOUR REASONING

13. The Houyhnhms do not think that Gulliver is a full Yahoo because
    a) he can talk b) he is intelligent c) he thinks that the Yahoos are disgusting d) all of the above.

14. When Gulliver returns to England, he lives in his own stables because
    a) he is still trying to be like a Houyhnhnm b) they are cleaner than his house c) there are no humans there d) his wife no longer welcomes him at home.

15. Gulliver ends his tale with a plea for truth because
    a) lying is a sin b) he always tells the truth c) the truth is more interesting than lies d) truth is important and valuable.

THINKING IT OVER

16. The author demonstrates that people are not very different from Yahoos. Find instances in the text where Yahoos act like people, and vice versa.

17. The author tells us that Houyhnhnms care for their children and take mates in a more sensible way than people or Yahoos do. Find evidence to support this reasoning in the text.

18. Gulliver is attacked by the natives of the island. Yet, he would rather take his chances there than return to England. He has a reason. Find this reason in the final chapter.